CONCILIUM

THEOLOGY IN THE AGE OF RENEWAL

CONCILIUM

CONCILIUM/VOL. 34

ECUMENICAL THEOLOGY

APOSTOLIC SUCCESSION
RETHINKING A BARRIER TO UNITY

edited by HANS KÜNG

VOLUME 34

CONCILIUM
theology in the age of renewal

PAULIST PRESS
NEW YORK, N.Y. / GLEN ROCK, N.J.

The Imprimatur for this volume applies
only to articles by Roman Catholic authors.

NIHIL OBSTAT: John E. Brooks, S.J., S.T.D.
Censor Deputatus

IMPRIMATUR: ✠ Bernard J. Flanagan, D.D.
Bishop of Worcester

March 28, 1968

The Nihil Obstat and Imprimatur are official declarations that a book or
pamphlet is free of doctrinal or moral error. No implication is contained
therein that those who have granted the Nihil Obstat and Imprimatur agree
with the contents, opinions or statements expressed.

Library of Congress Catalogue Card Number: 68–25948

Suggested Decimal Classification: 280.1

Paulist Press assumes responsibility for the accuracy of the English trans-
lations in this Volume.

PAULIST PRESS
EXECUTIVE OFFICES: 304 W. 58th Street, New York, N.Y. and 21 Harris-
town Road, Glen Rock, N.J.
Executive Publisher: John A. Carr, C.S.P.
Executive Manager: Alvin A. Illig, C.S.P.
Asst. Executive Manager: Thomas E. Comber, C.S.P.

EDITORIAL OFFICES: 304 W. 58th Street, New York, N.Y.
Editor: Kevin A. Lynch, C.S.P.
Managing Editor: Urban P. Intondi

Printed and bound in the United States of America by
The Colonial Press Inc., Clinton, Mass.

CONTENTS

PREFACE 1
       Hans Küng/Tübingen, W. Germany
           Translated by
          Theodore L. Westow

PART I

ARTICLES

THE TWELVE APOSTLES 5
      Béda Rigaux, O.F.M./Brussels, Belgium
           Translated by
          John H. Stevenson

NOTES ON THE TRADITIONAL TEACHING
ON APOSTOLIC SUCCESSION 16
      Antonio Javierre, S.D.B./Rome, Italy
           Translated by
           Paul Burns

WHAT IS THE ESSENCE OF
APOSTOLIC SUCCESSION? 28
      Hans Küng/Tügingen, W. Germany
           Translated by
          Theodore L. Westow

APOSTOLIC SUCCESSION: AN ATTRIBUTE
OF THE WHOLE CHURCH 36
      Johannes Remmers/Münster, W. Germany
           Translated by
          John Drury

THE SUCCESSION OF PROPHETS IN THE CHURCH 52
      Avery Dulles, S.J./Woodstock, Md.

IS THERE A "SUCCESSION OF TEACHERS"?   63
        Arnold van Ruler/Utrecht, Netherlands
            Translated by
           Theodore L. Westow

IS THERE A DOGMATIC DISTINCTION
BETWEEN THE FUNCTION OF PRIESTS
AND THE FUNCTION OF BISHOPS?   74
        Bernard Dupuy, O.P./Etiolles, France
            Translated by
             John Drury

CAN THERE BE APOSTOLIC SUCCESSION
OUTSIDE THE CHAIN OF IMPOSITION
OF HANDS?   87
        Maurice Villain, S.M./Paris, France
            Translated by
           Theodore L. Westow

WHAT CAN THE LAYMAN DO
WITHOUT THE PRIEST? 105
        Joseph Duss-von Werdt/Zurich, Switzerland
            Translated by
            Rev. Edward Quinn

WOMEN AS PRIESTS? 115
        Elizabeth Gössmann/Munich, W. Germany
            Translated by
             Simon King

IS THERE ROOM FOR WOMEN IN THE
FUNCTIONS OF THE CHURCH? 126
        Jan Peters, O.C.D./Smakt-Venray, Netherlands
            Translated by
           Theodore L. Westow

PART II

BIBLIOGRAPHICAL SURVEY

THE DISCUSSION ABOUT ANGLICAN ORDERS
IN MODERN ANGLICAN THEOLOGY 141
        Henry Chadwick/Oxford, England

THE ORTHODOX CHURCHES
AND ANGLICAN ORDERS 150
        Hilaire Marot, O.S.B./Chevetogne, France
            Translated by
             John Drury

PART III

DOCUMENTATION CONCILIUM
Office of the Executive Secretary
Nijmegen, Netherlands

WOMEN'S PLACE IN THE MINISTRY OF
NON-CATHOLIC CHRISTIAN CHURCHES 163
Concilium General Secretariat/Nijmegen, Netherlands
Translated by
Theodore L. Westow

BIOGRAPHICAL NOTES 179

Preface

Hans Küng/ *Tübingen, W. Germany*

It would be easier to accept a difference of opinion on apostolic succession in theory if it were not burdened with so many consequences in practice. To mention the most important element: one cannot overlook the fact that the main reason for the absence of intercommunion between Christians lies in the question of apostolic succession. Many reason that without a "valid" apostolic succession there is no valid ecclesiastical office; without a valid ecclesiastical office there can be no valid eucharist; without this valid office in other communities there can be no common celebration. And what is said about the importance of apostolic succession for the eucharist also holds, *mutatis mutandis,* for the whole organization of the Churches. There have been enough theologians who have made the application of the term "Church" to a particular community depend on the validity of apostolic succession.

All Churches have, in one way or another, their pastors, teachers and prophets. But to understand the meaning of their services at present, the respective interpretation of their succession and their relation to the origin of these services is of utmost importance. Here one of the essential features is that each service must preserve the value of its specific function for the community. And in this way it may be possible to bring about a fuller understanding of succession and to disentangle it from the juridical and

1

clerical narrowness that has restricted its meaning in the course of time, partly through the polemical and increasingly exclusive use made of the term. This is the purpose of this volume. The aim is to distinguish the enduring essence from the changing expressions on the basis of the original character, so that we can see the possibilities for a better realization of the Church's service today.

Ultimately we may come to see that the idea of apostolic succession expresses what is common to the various Churches rather than what divides them: the succession, not only of the apostles, but also of the prophets and the teachers, and, finally, of all the charismatic functions as the expression of the will of all the Churches to remain true to the Gospel and to let the apostolic message be expressed anew every day. Then orderly apostolic succession will express the will of all the Churches to live by the message of the apostles and their Lord, not as an anarchical, self-opinionated, autonomous and merely incidental agglomeration of different people, but as the orderly, obedient, faithful and serving community of Jesus Christ. The manner in which this is worked out will show how faithful every Church is to the Gospel. This is bound to have its effect on the brotherhood of the individual Churches. All the Churches have to face this eminently critical issue of how to be apostolic through succession.

PART I
ARTICLES

Béda Rigaux, O.F.M. / *Brussels, Belgium*

The Twelve Apostles

The subject of this article raises two questions: that of "the Twelve" in the primitive tradition and that of the title "apostle". For purposes of this present volume of *Concilium,* we are concerned only with the second, the title "apostle".

A little should first be said on the term *"apostolos"* itself. Its Greek root (*apostellein,* to send), gives no hint as to why the term *"apostolos"* in Greek means ship or fleet or finally admiral. The noun is found once only in the LXX (1 Kgs. 14, 6). *"Apostolos"* is a Christian word that must take its origin from the Church of Antioch where believers received the name of "Christians" (Acts 11, 26).[1]

[1] L. Cerfaux, "Pour l'histoire du titre *Apostolos* dans le Nouveau Testament," in *Rech. Sc. Rel.,* 48 (1960) pp. 76–92. The literature on this subject shows its current importance: K. H. Rengsdorf, *"Apostolos,"* in *Theol. Worterb. z. N.T.,* I (1933), pp. 406–46; J. L. McKenzie, "Apostle," in *Dict. of the Bible* (London, 1966), pp. 46–48; J. Wageman, *Die Stellung des Apostels Paulus neben den Zwölf in den ersten Jahrhunderten* (Leipzig, 1926), pp. 3–31; J. Rademakers, "Mission et apostolat," in *Studia Evang.,* 2 (Berlin, 1964), pp. 100–21; F. G. Gavin, "Shaliach und Apostolos," in *Anglic. Theol. Rev.,* 9 (1926–7), pp. 250–59; K. Lake, "The Twelve and the Apostles," in F. J. Foakes Jackson and L. Lake, *The Beginnings of Christianity,* Vol. I, *The Acts of the Apostles* (London, ⁵1933), pp. 257–303; P. Morant, "Zur Apostelzahl," in *Theol. prakt. Quart.,* 87 (1934), pp. 98–107; K. H. Rengsdorf, *Apostolat und Predigtamt. Ein Beitrag zur neutestamentlichen Grundlegung einer Lehre von Amt der Kirche* (Stuttgart, 1934); E. Barnikol, "Apos-

As for deriving both word and institution from the Hebrew
shaliah or the Aramaic *shaluah*, recent studies tend to reinforce
their distinctness rather than their relationship. The Book of
Chronicles gives evidence that men were "sent" to teach the Law

---

tel," in *Theologische Jahrbücher*, 10 (1942), pp. 40–47; H. Bruston, "La
notion d'apostolat dans l'Eglise primitive," in *Revue de Theologie et
d'Action evangelique*, 3 (1943), pp. 177–92; L. Cerfaux, "Témoins du
Christ d'après le Livre des Actes," in *Angelicum* 20 (1943), pp. 166–83;
H. von Campenhausen, "Der urchristliche Apostelbegriff," in *Studia
Theologica*, I (1947), pp. 96–130; H. Mosbeeh, "Apostolos in the New
Testament," in *Studia Theologica*, 2 (1948), pp. 166–200; A. Verheul,
"De moderne exegese over "αποστολσς" in *Sacris Erudiri*, 1 (1948), pp.
390–96; *idem*, "Kent Sint Paulus buiten 'de Twaalf' nog andere apostelen,"
in *Studia Catholica*, 22 (1947), pp. 65–75; 23 (1948), pp. 147–57, 217–
29; *idem*, "Proeve van een verklaring van II Cor., X–XIII," in *Sacris
Erudiri*, 2 (1949), pp. 5–43; *idem*, "Apostolaat en Verrijzenis: Onderzoek
naar de inhoud van iet apostelbegrip in I Cor.," in *Studia Catholica*, 26
(1951), pp. 171–84; E. Lohse, "Ursprung und Prägung des christlichen
Apostolats," in *Theol. Zeitschr.*, 9 (1953), pp. 259–75; L. Cerfaux,
"L'unite du corps apostolique dans le N.T.," in *Melanges Lambert
Beauduin* (Chevetogne, 1954); E. M. Kredel, "Der Apostelbegriff in der
neuesten Exegese. Historisch-kritische Darstellung," in *Zeitschr. f. kathol.
Theol.*, 78 (1956), pp. 169–93, 257–305; J. Colson, "Les fonctions
ecclésiales aux deux premiers siècles," in *Textes et etudes theologiques*
(Bruges-Paris, 1956); C. K. Barrett, "The Apostles in and after the New
Testament," in *Svenk Exegetisk Årsbok* 21 (1957), pp. 30–49; H. Stirni-
mann, "Apostelamt und Apostolische Ueberlieferung," in *Freib. Zeitschr.
f. Phil. und Theol.*, 4 (1957), pp. 129–47; W. Schmithals, *Das kirchliche
Apostelamt. Eine historische Untersuchung* (Göttingen, 1961); G. Klein,
Der Ursprung des Zwölferapostolats. Ursprung und Gestalt einer Idee"
(Göttingen, 1961); P. Blaeser, "Zum Problem des urchristlichen Apostolats," in *Unio Christ.* (Paderborn, 1962); H. Agneu, "La notion neo-
testamentaire d'apostolos selon la critique moderne," in *Diss* (Fribourg/
Switzerland, 1963); N. Mulde, "La mission des apotres," in *Christus* 10
(1963), pp. 450–60; W. Schneemelcher, *Neutestamentliche Apokriphen
in deutscher Uebersetzung*, 3 (Tübingen, [3]1964): articles by W. Schneemelcher (pp. 5–10), W. Bauer (pp. 11–41), M. Hornschuh (pp. 41–52);
H. Rottmann, "Der Apostolat Pauli nach I Kor. 15 und Gal. 1. u. 2," in
Igrejia Luterana, 24 (1963), pp. 225–42; B. Gerhardsson, "Die Boten
Gottes und die Apostel Christi," in *Sv. Ex. Ar.*, 27 (1962), pp. 89–121;
L. Cerfaux, "La mission apostolique des Douze et sa portée eschato-
logique," in *Mélanges E. Tisserant*, I (Vatican City, 1964), pp. 43–66;
E. Klostermann, "Noch einmal uber Paulus zum Apostelamt," in *Wissen-
schaftl. Zeitschr.*, 13 (1964), pp. 149–50; J. Knox, "Rom. 15, 14–33 and
Paul's Conception of His Apostolic Mission," in *Journ. of Bibl. Lit.* 83
(1964), pp. 1–11.

(2 Chr. 17, 7–9). Rabbinic usage applies the term to those whom the Jerusalem Sanhedrin used to send to the Jews of the Diaspora. Their function was to establish the calendar, collect gifts, visit local communities, nominate teachers and maintain contact between the Diaspora and Palestine. But this rabbinic evidence all dates from after 70 A.D., the first being probably around 140 A.D. These missionaries received a laying on of hands and the man designated to pray in the name of the community is called "sent"; but this title is never given to one working to make proselytes. The rabbis lay special emphasis on four who were "sent": Moses, Elijah, Elisha and Ezekiel, whose miracle-working proved that they were sent by God. It is thus clear that there is only a very tenuous likeness between the *shaliah* and the apostle.[2]

I

THE SYNOPTICS

Let us now turn to the New Testament usage of the word. In a few passages it is used to designate a simple messenger (2 Cor. 8, 23); the same sense is retained in passages associating prophets with apostles (Lk. 11, 49; Eph. 3, 5; Apoc. 2, 2 and 18, 20). There is no question here of a technical title. When we turn to the Synoptics the word "apostle" in the strong sense is found twice in Mark, once in Matthew, six times in Luke. There seems no point in re-examining this usage. One can, on the whole, adopt the conclusions of J. Dupont: "If one does no violence to the gospel texts, they do not allow us to assert nor even to suppose that Jesus, in his earthly life, gave to the Twelve this title

---

[2] The derivation of *apostolos* from the Jewish institution of the *sheluhim* owed its momentary success to the works of K. G. Rengsdorf. For criticism, see A. Ehrardt, *The Apostolic Succession in the First Two Centuries of the Church* (London, 1953); H. Mosbeeh, *Apostolos*, pp. 168ff; L. Cerfaux, *Pour l'histoire*, p. 185; W. Schmithals, *op. cit.*, pp. 92–99; G. Klein, *op. cit.*, pp. 26–27.

of apostles as one proper to themselves." Even in Luke, the intention "does not seem to be to inform the reader on the origin of the term 'apostolos' but rather to point out to him that the disciples in question are the apostles".[3]

II

THE ACTS

The term "apostle" is therefore a creation of the primitive Church and must be considered within the milieu where it originated. There is no doubt that, as far as the gospel of St. Luke and the Acts are concerned, the Twelve are referred to by the simple formula, "the apostles". This terminology appears also in the editorial passages such as Acts 1, 2—they are chosen by Jesus—and in the "summaries" that show them teaching and presiding (Acts 2, 42–43)—bearing witness to the resurrection (4, 33), presiding over the distribution of property (Acts 4, 34–37; cf. 5, 2), performing signs and miracles (Acts 5, 12), giving the Spirit (8, 18; 15, 28). Elsewhere they speak in the name of Jesus (5, 40), lay their hands on the seven deacons (6, 6), or else are mentioned as remaining in Jerusalem (8, 1. 14; 11, 1). In every case the reference is clearly to the Twelve but the Acts bear witness to another phenomenon; Paul and Barnabas receive the title of apostles (Acts 14, 4. 14) and in several cases "the apostles and the elders" represent authority in the Church of Jerusalem (15, 2. 4. 6. 22. 23; 16, 4). This last expression goes back to the source used by Luke. In the three accounts of the vocation of Paul, he is not named "apostle"; he calls himself one "sent" by the Lord Jesus (9, 7; 22, 21; 26, 17). This silence and the uniqueness of the case in which *"apostoloi"*

---

[3] J. Dupont, *Le nom d'apôtres*, pp. 46–47. Dupont's conclusion is not admitted by K. H. Rengsdorf, who refers to "Shaliach", *art. cit.*, p. 429, and is called into doubt by E. Haenchen in *Der Weg Jesu*, pp. 247–48, at least as far as concerns Mark.

does refer to Paul and Barnabas leads one to think that in these two passages Luke did not employ the word in the strong sense; Paul and Barnabas are "sent" by the Church of Antioch.

It therefore seems clear that, insofar as the Lucan redactions of the gospel and the Acts are concerned, "the Twelve" have become "the apostles". On the other hand, this changeover does not come about as the result of any new definition or mission. Their election, their power, their mission are based, in the most ancient evangelical tradition, on their relationship to Jesus as the Twelve. The Acts are evidence that the Church was becoming aware of all that was implied by the status of apostle; they had to have been with the Lord the whole time that he lived among us, and, above all, they had to have been witnesses of how he was taken away so as to be witnesses of his resurrection (Acts 1, 21–22).[4] Moreover, by virtue of their election, the apostles are the heirs of Jesus' power (5, 12); they confer the gift of the Spirit (8, 18) and associate their own authority with that of the Spirit (15, 28). Their ministry is to speak "in the name of Jesus" (5, 40). Their activities as authorities within the Church, teaching, presiding, the laying on of hands, the appointment of deacons, are simply manifestations of this continuity.

The substitution of "the apostles" for "the Twelve" seems therefore to be the introduction rather of a new term than of a new fact. What is new is the whole post-Easter situation, comprising the resurrection and the organizing of believers into a community of prayer, of teaching, of charity, a community that possesses the Spirit and in which there exists a recognized authority.[5]

---

[4] See Ph. H. Menoud, "Jésus et ses témoins. Remarques sur L'unité de l'oeuvre de Luc," in *Eglise et Théologie* (privately printed): "Only the apostles are the witnesses of Christ. . . . [Paul] is therefore a witness in the eyes of the author of the Acts" (pp. 7–8).

[5] Luke is preoccupied with the extension of Christianity by prominent individuals and not with the exercise of authority by the Twelve. If he shows the apostles in action, or even in assembly, it is always in a ministry of mission, of expansion. Cf. W. Mundle, "Das Apostelbild der Apostelgeschichte," in *Zeitschr f. d. Neutest. Wiss.*, 27 (1928), pp. 36–54.

III

St. Paul

Let us now turn to St. Paul.[6] Some do him the honor of believing that the notion of apostleship was his creation. It is perfectly true that the epistles are older than the Synoptics and the Acts. The word "apostle" occurs no less than 34 times in the epistles. In the light of recent studies we can group our observations under two headings: (1) Is the title "apostle" reserved to the Twelve? (2) What qualifications are needed to be an "apostle"?

1. We can pass rapidly over the case of Silvanus and Timothy, who, in 1 Timothy 2, 5–7, are associated with Paul as "apostles of Christ" and over that of Sosthenes and Apollos who are similarly associated in 1 Corinthians 4, 9. It is a question of "missionaries". Are Andronicos and Junias named "apostles" in Romans 16, 7? The matter is uncertain because one can translate "highly esteemed by the apostles" as opposed to "highly esteemed among the apostles".[7]

The case of Barnabas is unmistakable. He is an apostle just as Paul is: "Are Barnabas and I the only ones without the right not to work?" (1 Cor. 9, 6). Now, in the preceding verse Paul named as terms of comparison "the other apostles and the breth-

[6] J. Crocker, "The Apostolic Succession in the Light of the History of the Primitive Church," in *Anglic. Theol. Rev.*, 18 (1936), pp. 1–21; J. Munck, "Paul, the Apostles and the Twelve," in *Studia Theologica*, 3 (1949), pp. 96–110; J. M. Morris, *Paul's Claim and Concept of Apostleship. Significance in the New Testament* (Southern Baptist Theological Seminary, 1955); idem, "Paul's Understanding of Apostleship," in *The Review and Expositor*, 55 (1958), pp. 400–12; J. Roloff, *Apostolat-Verkundigung-Kirche. Ursprung, Inhalt und Funktion des Apostelamts nach Paulus, Lukas und den Pastoralbriefen* (Gütersloh, 1965); H. Rottmann, "Der Apostolat Pauli nach I Kor. 15 und Gal. I u. 2," in *Igrejia Luterana*, 24 (1963), pp. 225–42; E. Klostermann, "Noch einmal über Paulus zum Apostelamt," in *Wissenschaftl Zeitschr.*, 13 (1964), pp. 149–50; J. Knox, "Rom. 15, 14–33 and Paul's Conception of His Apostolic Mission," in *Journ. of Bibl. Lit.* 83 (1964), pp. 1–11; J. Rademakers, "Mission et apostolat dans l'évangile johannique," in *Studia Evangelica*, 2 (Berlin, 1964), pp. 100–21.

[7] Cf. J. Dupont, *Le nom d'apôtre*, p. 11 and the studies of A. Verheul and W. Schmithals, *Das kirchliche Apostelamt*, pp. 13–14.

ren of the Lord". It follows therefore that Barnabas must be recognized as an apostle. This passage of 1 Corinthians 9 raises the problem of the "brethren of the Lord": the fact that they are mentioned side by side with the apostles, whose prerogative it is to take a sister with them, forces us to conclude that these brethren of the Lord must themselves be counted among "the apostles".

James, the brother of the Lord, is himself an apostle. In 1 Corinthians 15, 7 Paul writes: "Thereafter he appeared to James, then to all the apostles." The Twelve are mentioned a moment before (15, 5). Verse 7 shows Paul abandoning the tradition whose terms he cites in 15, 5–6. Just as Cephas is one of the Twelve, James seems to be one of the apostles. This James was, at the time, head of the Church of Jerusalem. In Galatians 1, 19 Paul definitely seems to count him among the apostles: "I saw no other apostle, save only James, the brother of the Lord." Contemporary exegesis, on the whole, has given up the attempt to identify this James with James son of Alphaeus or James the Less. The group of the Twelve is absolutely distinct from the group of the Lord's brethren (Mk. 3, 31; Acts 1, 14; Jn. 2, 13; 7, 5). In spite of the doubts that may persist concerning the identity and number of the "apostles", the more probable conclusion is that "the apostles" are a wider group than the Twelve.

2. The authentic definition of the apostle in the light of what is said by Paul is very much more significant. Paul develops a real theology of this title.

He never counts himself among the Twelve. And nonetheless he constantly lays claim to his title of apostle. He bases his claim on his vision of the risen Christ at Damascus. If Jesus showed himself to "all the apostles" (1 Cor. 15, 7), he showed himself to Paul also (1 Cor. 15, 8–9). To the Corinthians Paul puts the question: "Am I not an apostle? Have I then not seen Jesus, our Lord?" (1 Cor. 9, 1). In the Epistle to the Galatians he makes the solemn declaration that "he, having called me by his grace, thought fit to reveal his Son to me so that I might proclaim him to the Gentiles" (Gal. 1, 16). This is echoed in the Epistle to the Romans; Paul has received his apostolic mission from Jesus Christ, our Lord, who, by his resurrection from the dead, has been constituted Son of God (Rom. 1, 4–5). This basis for his claiming the title of apostle is no more than a necessary condition; nowhere is it stated that the title belongs to all who saw the risen Christ. The vision on the road to Damascus is not necessarily Paul's election as an apostle.[8] But the apostle is a witness of what he has seen and heard. Can one not explain Paul's silence concerning the public life of Jesus in terms of one basic fact, namely, his refusal to bear witness to anything but what he had seen himself? He bears witness to the death and to the resurrection of Jesus, to his apparition in glory. He has no need of any ecclesiastical appointing in order to become an apostle. By the revelation of the risen Christ he is placed on the same footing as the Twelve, or almost so. His approaches to them at Jerusalem show clearly enough that he feels the need of a *koinonia,* of a unity, which he is bound to respect, in order not to run in vain.[9] However, there is more to Paul's consciousness of himself as an apostle than vision and witness.

At the very foundation of his calling as an apostle, Paul claims a divine predestination, clearly apparent in Galatians 1, 15–16 with its unmistakable use of Isaiah 49, 1 and Jeremiah 1, 5. He was chosen from his mother's womb and Christ makes of him a "servant" of Yahweh as he was himself.[10] God therefore intervenes by his own free initiative in his election, the unique experience that finds its consummation in the vision on the road to Damascus. It is this vision that qualified him to be a witness.[11] And it is by another divine initiative that the Gospel was confided to Paul: "Our God granted us to preach boldly before you the Gospel of God," he says to the Thessalonians (1 Thess. 2, 2), but this realization followed a choice and a mission: "We were thought worthy by God to have the Gospel confided to us," he

---

[8] Cf. B. Rigaux, "Saint Paul et ses lettres," in *Studia neotestamentica. Subsidia* 2 (Bruges-Paris, 1962), pp. 86–90.

[9] Gal. 2, 2. 10.

[10] B. Rigaux, *op. cit.,* pp. 83–86.

[11] *Ibid.,* pp. 69–77.

adds (1 Thess. 2, 4). The evidence available does not allow us to site in time the union between the vision and the mission of Paul, above all, his mission to the Gentiles. Luke, in his accounts of Paul's vocation, has fused vision and vocation into a single tableau. There seem to be good grounds for agreeing with P. Gächter when he says: "In the vision that converted him, Paul received no mission and it was not then that he became the apostle of the Gentiles." [12] At Antioch his mission must have become clear (Gal. 2, 1–10). But for Paul, his election, his authority and his mission were bestowed on him by God and through the risen Christ.

IV

THE RISEN CHRIST

When the Church moved into her new post-Easter situation, there emerged a new dimension in the mission of the Twelve. We find it in the words of the risen Christ. The perspective in which Luke ends his first book is that of "preaching to all nations" (Lk. 24, 47). He began the Acts with: "You will be my witnesses at Jerusalem, throughout Judaea and Samaria and even to the ends of the earth" (Acts 1, 8). The command provisionally not to leave Jerusalem had in view the descent of the Spirit. In Matthew their mission takes on imposing dimensions; Jesus meets the eleven disciples on the mountain, dispels all doubts and utters the celebrated formula: "All power has been given to me in heaven and on earth; go therefore and make disciples of all nations" (28, 16–19). Finally, the fourth gospel bears witness to the same tradition: " 'Even as the Father sent me, I also send you.' When he had said this, he breathed on them and said to them: 'Receive the Holy Spirit. If you forgive the sins of any, they are forgiven; if you retain the sins of any, they are retained' " (Jn. 20, 21–23). In the same way as Luke, John associates the giving of the Spirit with their sending.

[12] P. G. Gächter, *Petrus und seine Zeit* (Innsbruck, 1958), p. 411.

V

RESULTS AND CONCLUSIONS

It is now time to draw a few conclusions.

1. The group of the Twelve goes back to the Galilean ministry of Jesus. It follows on the gathering of disciples, of individual vocations and fits into the context of the substitution of a new Israel for the old.

2. With the institution of the Twelve are associated election, vocation and also their being sent as missionaries throughout Galilee. The Twelve and their provisional mission were the prelude to the universal mission of the new economy. At the period of the Gospel's redaction, institution and mission had come to be seen within a broader context based on the development of an expanding Christianity. There is an intimate connection between the facts and their interpretation. That is why it is an error to divorce theology from the authenticity of the events in which it finds its origin and foundation.[13]

3. The apostleship is not a creation of St. Paul. The title of apostle and the formula "the twelve apostles" date from the period following the resurrection. They became loaded with all the significance contained in the formulas: the twelve disciples, the Twelve. The enrichment is due to the death and resurrection of Jesus. To be counted among the twelve apostles involved bearing witness to the words and deeds of Jesus' ministry and to the experience of his resurrection. To this was added the mission given them after the resurrection, which enlarged their first vocation. The significance of being "an apostle" is to be understood

---

[13] P. Batiffol, "L'Apostolat," in *Rev. Bibl.*, 3 (1906), pp. 520–32; "Apotres," in *Dict. Apol. de la Foi Cathol.*, I, pp. 251–61; L. Cerfaux, *La mission de Galilee*, p. 445: "It is almost certain that a primitive Gospel redaction (Mark in its ancient state) employed only the title ὁι μαθηταί ("the disciples") for the Twelve. This was how they were referred to before the death of our lord. The primitive community grew accustomed to say ὁι Τώδεκα ("the Twelve"), then ὁι ἀπόατολοι ("the apostles") and finally ὁι δωδεκα ἀπόατολοι ("the twelve apostles"). It is natural that Christian customs should have reacted on the Gospel formulae, introducing into them, above all in our section (that of the Galilee mission), a later vocabulary."

in terms of two closely connected elements: to have seen the risen Christ and to have been sent out by him. This explains the formation of a second class of apostles, no less authorized than the first, although fellowship with the Twelve was experienced as a necessity.

4. The creation of a group of Twelve and the apostleship in the primitive Church is not a simple question of names or of facts without theological bearing. R. Bultmann is very close to the truth when he asserts that the Twelve "are characteristic of the community's eschatological consciousness".[14] By the preaching of the kingdom of God men were led to an expectation of the end. Their ignorance of when and how the end would come divided their minds between the feeling that the end was near and the necessity to take account of the realities of daily life. Their faith in the resurrection of Jesus, the coming down of the Spirit, the proclamation of the presence of the glorified Lord in the bosom of the Christian communities had not changed, in the men who had followed and been chosen by him, their certitude of having been the chosen, the called, the men sent and commissioned to continue and to proclaim the kingdom of God. This consciousness of the calling received before the resurrection was vivified by the mission given to them after it established that continuity which guaranteed the permanence of the new religious economy. The formulas underwent an evolution, but the reality took root and adapted itself to new conditions. That is the way the Church is built, the city of God. At the end of the 1st century, the seer could write: "The wall of the city rests on twelve foundations, each bearing the name of one of the twelve apostles of the Lamb" (Apoc. 21, 14).

[14] R. Bultmann, "Theologie des Neuen Testaments," in *Neue Theologische Grundrisse* (Tübingen, 1958), p. 40.

Antonio Javierre, S.D.B. / *Rome, Italy*

Notes on the Traditional Teaching on Apostolic Succession

Nothing could be more appropriate today than a few thoughts on this theme. First, because of its permanent value in dogmatic theology. The article of the Creed "I believe in one . . . apostolic Church" alludes to a definite derivation from the apostles. This, in Catholic thinking, comes about through succession.

Second, because of the prominent place it occupies in the debates that have taken place during this century. This is a century of longing for unity and strenuous efforts to achieve it. These efforts have been stymied by the problem of succession. At the inaugural conference in Lausanne it was already a problem under the heading of Faith and Order; it is still unresolved, to judge from the reports of the Theological Congress of Montreal.

Third, because of the urgent need to rephrase the statement of the problem. Vatican II demands that this be done without delay. It offers new elements that make this possible, and at the same time indicates the methodology to be followed. It is no longer permissible to dig oneself into entrenched positions that threaten to nullify the immense advantages to be gained from the dialogue that is taking place today.

So, by way of response to these demands, let us try, even if rather sketchily, to: (1) outline the contours of the problem as seen through the traditional debates; (2) work out its exact coordinates at the present moment; (3) suggest the most promising course for the dialogue of the future to follow.

I

TRADITIONAL POSING OF THE PROBLEM

I am referring to a ten-year-old paper of mine which sets out all the elements of the problem.[1] It has the merit, at least, of giving a bird's eye view of the whole immensely complex question.

1. There is not a single Christian confession which is not involved in the struggle. This is not just accidental. It is because apostolic succession of some sort is a basic condition for the very existence of Christian communities, to the extent that it serves as an ideal criterion for their comparative classification.

Looking at the spectrum from left to right, so to speak, we find confessions radically *opposed* to the idea of succession; those in favor of the transmission of *doctrine* alone; some who would extend acceptance to include the *ministry*; "catholic" confessions which also require the collegial succession of *bishops*; and, finally, Rome, which adds the *pope* as the head of the college of bishops.

Through terminology which is often very confused, there are glimpses of a robust outline of reality. Amsterdam summed it up in the famous diagram of the two lines meeting at right angles: Catholicism favoring the *horizontal* of hereditary transmission, in complete contrast to the strict *verticality* of Protestantism. This is coming close to caricature, but contains perfectly objective insights.

2. Where do the opponents concentrate their attack?

(a) They flatly reject the *apologetic* value of succession. They would not consider the mere fact of having an uninterrupted list of bishops in the archives as sufficient credentials to establish the ecclesial reality of a Church. They would regard this as an

---

[1] A. Ma. Javierre, "Cuestiones debatidas hoy," in *XVI^a Sem. Esp. Theol.* (Madrid, 1957), pp. 3–96.

unacceptably mechanical claim and even a scandalous subordination of the Word to those who should be putting themselves at its service.

(b) The attack in the *dogmatic* field is three-pronged, with each prong more or less complementary to the others. First, the *exegetes* claim that they can find no trace of it in the Bible: no *apostolos* to be succeeded, no *episcopos* resembling a hierarchical bishop, and no theme of *diadoche* (succession) to start them off. Second, the *historians* deny any continuity between the foundation period and post-apostolic institutions. They condemn the *diadoche* idea in particular because of its uncertain parentage. Its late appearance is for them an argument that it originated as a counter-claim made by nascent Catholicism in the face of the dangerous claims of the Gnostics. Finally, the *theologians*: they show that the supposed link between apostles and bishops produces the following dilemma—either the two institutions are homogeneous, in which case the idea of a genuine, unrepeatable *apostle* goes up in smoke, or they are heterogeneous, which leads to a devaluation of the *diadoche's* claim to a strict continuity. The most they could concede would be a succession of bishops, but by no means an apostolic succession.

So the opposition could hardly be more deep-rooted. It violently attacks the three key points of succession: the *personal* element (apostles-bishops), the *real* element (the apostolic deposit), and the *formal* element (formed by a delicate interplay of relations between the deposit and the depositaries).

This was the position about twenty years ago. We must now see what has happened since then to make the contemporary debate somewhat different in content.

II

PRESENT ORIENTATIONS

A look through the publications of the last decade[2] gives an

---

[2] I have in mind studies by Benoît, Blum, Bonnard, Colson, Congar,

impression of distinct progress. This is not only because of the more ironic tone prevailing, but because of the genuine new contributions that have been made, some most valuable.

The thesis of succession, suitably moderated, does not cause quite the scandal it used to.[3] The divine origin of the ministry is very commonly recognized.[4] Some "non-Catholic" writers do not hide their nostalgia, as ministers, for unity in descent from the apostles.[5] Some even study sacramental ordination with serenity and frank sympathy.[6] Others try out formulas of equivalence, in the hope of localizing the function of bishop, in the dogmatic sense, in places where sociological conditions would not seem to admit its existence.[7]

It would be excessive to consider every point in detail here; let us just run rapidly through the main areas of change.

1. Progress must be attributed, above all, to the historical setting in which the problem has been placed. Theology in general has tended to ignore history far too much; in a field as essentially historical as this one—apostolic *succession*—the lack of an historical focus could only be fatal. Should the impulse provided by existentialism be seen at the back of this new emphasis on history? Or is it rather a natural reaction of Christianity when attacked in its very essentials? Whatever the cause, the important thing is that the historical approach is today a fortunate fact. Its influence is generally highly beneficial, at least on this subject.

(a) History seems to have overcome a dialectical tension that is very dangerous in apologetics, at a time when there seemed to

---

Fincke, Frei, Cassman, Hall, Javierre, Karrer, Kinder, Küng, Lerche, Margot, Martelet, Milburn, Ratzinger, Schlink, Schillig, Scipioni, Stadler, Stählin, von Balthasar, von Heyl, etc.

[3] Cf. E. Schlink "La succession apostolique," in *Verbum Caro,* 69 (1964), pp. 52–86.

[4] Cf. recent symposia: *Das Amt der Einheit* (Stuttgart, 1964); *Ministère et Laicat* (*Verbum Caro,* 71–2, 1964).

[5] E. Fincke, "Das Amt der Einheit," *op. cit.,* pp. 77–190.

[6] M. Thurian, "L'ordination des pasteurs," in *Verbum Caro,* 57 (1961), pp. 199–213.

[7] J. J. von Allmen, "Le ministère des anciens. Essai sur le probleme du presbytérat en ecclésiologie réformée," in *Min. et Laicat,* pp. 214–56.

be no dialogue possible between the two camps—those for whom the word judges the institution and their opposites.

There is no longer, in particular, a sustained attack on the principle of institution: to support a given deposit on the basis of succession is not an arbitrary and late development, as its adversaries would claim. The formula *paradosis kata diadochen* reflects a very rich literary vein of undeniable antiquity, which has had a profound influence on the formation of the Christian ethos. There is nothing strange in the first Christian writers using the categories of their contemporaries, and even adapting the dominant thought processes to the new realities of Christianity.[8]

On the other hand, to admit the legitimacy of the principle does not mean unreservedly canonizing any apologetic application of it. Some of these frankly abuse it. Historians are well aware that a Hellenistic *paradosis* submitted to the normal coming and going of transmission will show a number of variations. Why not take this into account in apologetics? There is not sufficient ground in the Hellenistic mechanism for the absolute immutability attributed to the revealed deposit. This would be an undue limitation of its possibilities. To uphold it requires support of a kind that history cannot provide.

(b) When we come to the purely dogmatic field, there is now a greater respect for the demands of the positive data in evidence.

(i.) *Theologians* no longer impose arbitrary definitions. And, once the classic concept is accepted, most of the objections disappear: the *singularity* of the apostolate—did not the ancients talk of "pythagoric succession" and *diadochoi* of Alexander the Great?—and the *difference in degree* between apostle and bishop. Succession rests on analogy; identity between successor and succeeded is not indispensable—strictly speaking, it is not even possible.

(ii.) The *exegetes,* too, are refining the expression of their position. They recognize that there is nothing repugnant about

---

[8] On the whole of this problem, cf. A. Ma. Javierre, *El tema literario de la sucesión. Prologómenos para el estudio de la sucesión apostólica* (Zurich, 1963).

succession divorced from its technical refinements. They are finding synonyms that show it in a better light. There is a particular reason for not using the term *diadoche,* in that it carries the idea of an already established succession, and therefore has no place in a New Testament framework dominated by the presence and activity of the apostles. But even if the term itself is not used, denial of the idea is now not taken to excessive lengths. There is nothing against prophetic formulations of the idea of succession.

2. The advance that has been made thanks to the contribution of the historical approach still leaves us far short of the ultimate goal.[9] How far can the dogmatic theologians be held responsible for the slow rate of advance?

(a) The efforts directed at making the place of the *Spirit* stand out clearly in the process of succession are the ones that deserve particular praise; they are pointing in the right direction. Apostolic succession shares in the mystery of Christ. Therefore, it is right to trace its corporeal element in the Hellenistic world, provided that the full richness of its Spirit-inspired content is not forgotten.[10]

(b) The approach to the subject through the key of *apostolicity* is rather more problematic.[11] In view of the deep relationship between apostolicity and succession, it would be good if the study of the former could lend depth to the theme of the latter.

[9] It is enough to mention the official statements: in Germany, *Erklärung zur apostolischen Sukzession,* by the Ecumenical Committee of the Evangelical Churches (*Inf. der VELKD,* Märzheft, 1958), pp. 4–13; in France, *Luthériens et Réformés (Foi et Vie,* 1958), pp. 411–16.

[10] Y. Congar, "Apostolicité de ministère et apostolicité de doctrine. Réaction protestante et Tradition Catholique," in *Volk Gottes* (Freiburg im Br., 1967), pp. 84–111.

[11] Fincke, *art. cit.,* pp. 155ff., reproaches Schlink for the union he makes of the two themes. But the latter does not in fact confuse them; he juxtaposes them: "The two things are indissolubly linked. This is why our theme also has to be precisely defined: apostolic succession of the Church and of the ecclesial ministry. It is only when these two points are taken in conjunction that it is possible to see clearly what ecclesiological value can be given to the special question of apostolic succession, conceived as the unbroken chain of the laying-on of hands by the bishops" (*art. cit.,* p. 53). Not all authors are so circumspect in not reducing the two subjects to one: apostolicity.

There are unfortunately too many studies that fail to get to the root of the matter because they are not sufficiently broadly based. To make apostolicity the central ground of the approach would be a splendid corrective. The worry would be that this approach could become a pretext for burying a theme that is a source of disagreement in our ecumenical relations. To reduce apostolic succession to a generic succession of the whole Church would merely be skirting the problem, with a whole trail of attendant misunderstandings.

(i.) The *diadoche* is an essential *organ* in the structures of the Church, as well as a *criterion* of truth. In Catholic ecclesiology, apostolic succession becomes something similar to the functions attributed to the miracles of Christ in revelation: they are the *Word,* and also the *countersign,* of God. There was a time when studies of the miracles as well as of succession seemed to be the exclusive preserve of the apologists. The science of theology suffered seriously as a result. Fortunately, dogmatic theology has now energetically reclaimed its rights. Today there are solid Catholic monographs on miracles from a theological point of view, and it is to be hoped that one will soon be able to say the same of succession. However, one does not, of course, want to fall into the opposite trap: that dogmatics should encroach too far into the field of fundamental theology. Just as a purely dogmatic treatment is insufficient to deal fully with the purely apologetic aspect of miracles, so the mere fact of approaching the *diadoche* from the focus of apostolicity is insufficient to clarify every unknown criterion concerning it. They are complementary aspects, but formally distinct, and not to be confused.

(ii.) The equivocation likewise extends into the purely dogmatic field. The apostles were the first disciples of Christ, and the Church perpetuates the attitude of the Twelve, squatting at the feet of their master. From this point of view it is permissible to assert that it is the whole Church that is the successor of the apostolic college. But the apostles had a particular mission, and apostolic succession, in the strict sense, aspires precisely to perpetuate this mission of being vicars of Christ. So there is, one might say, succession and succession, just as there is the common priesthood of all the faithful and the ministerial priesthood, and they are specifically different from one another.[12] Apostolicity and strict apostolic succession are likewise intimately linked to one another, but also specifically different from one another—so much so that while one is an article of faith, the other is a real stumbling block in ecumenical relations.

III

LOOKING TO THE FUTURE

The simple confrontation of facts suggests the best strategy to be followed. Dialogue, centered on the Bible, should base itself on history and dogmatic theology in order to outline the concept of succession and determine its constituents.

Holy Scripture offers numerous starting points. The verse (Jn. 20, 21) with which Vatican II opened its theological statement on bishops seems particularly promising: "As the Father has sent me, even so I send you." [13]

This is not usually quoted in the context of succession. Nevertheless, this use has a very ancient foundation and interesting reflections in the theology of the reformed tradition.[14] This exe-

---

[12] Vatican II expressedly recalls this difference in the *Constitution on the Church,* n. 10. Von Allmen insists on this, in "Montréal, 1963", in *Verbum Caro,* 69 (1964), pp. 101–2.

[13] Vatican II, *Decree on the Pastoral Office of Bishops in the Church,* n. 1.

[14] The theologian Francisco Torres inferred succession from the *logion,* arguing thus: "For the Lord said, 'As my Father sent . . .' but the Father had sent Christ with the power of sending the apostles, so the apostles were empowered to send others. Christ, when he sent the apostles, gave them the Holy Spirit, saying: 'Receive the Holy Spirit'; so the apostles did the same and their successors do the same, else they themselves were not sent as the Father had sent Christ" (*Apud Theiner, II,* p. 144). R. Paquier, of the Swiss Reformed Church, also reads something similar in the text: " 'As the Father has sent me . . .' Jesus' delegation of the messianic powers to the Twelve seems to require, as its normal explanation, a chain of continuous transmission from them to others, from generation to generation, for as long as the present economy lasts": "Le prob-

gesis could appear mistaken on the grounds that we should reject apostolic succession by the very force of the analogy between Christ and his apostles, since there is no succession of Christ. But this inference is really out of court. Ancient tradition puts the *diadoche* forward as the means of leveling out the time lag between the deposit and the depositary. When the balance between them is perfect, as in Christ, succession is redundant; but when the depositaries, apostles, are mortal and the deposit, apostolicity, is permanent, then, in the minds of all the ancient writers, succession is indispensable.

There is, therefore, no argument. The law is always the same, although circumstances have given it opposing applications.

But does it in fact make any sense to talk of apostolic succession? It suggests the idea that something apostolic can be multiplied *ad infinitum,* and is it permissible to drag the apostle from his framework in this way?

Christ's *logion* continues: "Receive the Holy Spirit. If you forgive the sins of any, they are forgiven. . . ." Here the true outline of an apostle is drawn: he is a *speaker* of the Word and a *dispenser* of the mysteries.

The apostolic mission, basic to the Church, relates in several ways to the two trinitarian mysteries of the Word and the Spirit.[15] The apostles straddle these two phases of salvation history: they serve Christ in the last years of his life on earth, and they are instruments of the Spirit in the first manifestations stemming from Pentecost.

Once this is accepted, what meaning can be attached to apostolic succession? Once the apostles were dead, their successors

---

lème oecuménique du ministère," in *La Succession apostolique* (Lausanne, 1937), p. 8.

[15] N. Afanassieff takes a position completely contrary to that of Cullmann (who refers the apostolate to the time of the incarnation): "We have already seen that, in our view, the apostolate does not relate to the time of the incarnation but to that of the Church. This disposes of the principal argument of Cullman against 'apostolic succession' ": "L'Apôtre Pierre et l'évèque de Rome," in *Théologie,* 26 (1955), pp. 629–30. I believe both positions to be false, through the defect of excess.

had to continue their mission in perpetuity. As with any sort of succession, neither their personal traits nor the unique circumstances of their position could be handed on. But the succession did embrace everything that was capable of being carried down in history.

Personal relationship with Christ clearly had to cease with the Twelve. Their successors inherited the *deposit* but not the *ministry* of revelation. In terms of the Spirit, though, the inheritance was fuller, embracing not only the *content* of the dispensation but also the *function* of dispensing the mysteries. The reason for this is that the Spirit does not change in his manner of animating the Church.

So here at least is one continually self-multiplying apostolic aspect, exercised in the foundational period of the Church and permanent in value. Is this not what the *diadoche* strictly requires?

Let us, for the last time, set out the analogy to seek reasons which suggest that the bishop is the rightful inheritor of the title of successor to the apostles: "As my Father sent me. . . ." Is this a legitimate equation: bishops/apostles = apostles/Christ?

1. Of all the disciples of Christ, only twelve were chosen as his "official hearers". It was their task, in the name of the Church, to register the essential message of the master.

Since Christ is the Word (the whole Word and the Word of all, through his speeches, actions, silences, attitude, personality), it can be said that revelation continued as long as there was an apostle remaining who was capable of formulating details of the Word that they had the fortune to hear, see and touch (1 Jn. 1, 1).

Their position was also privileged in the realm of the Spirit. Even though the Spirit came down on the whole Church, he came down on the Cenacle in a particular way. Outside the Cenacle he illuminated men's minds; it was only the Twelve who were converted into infallible teachers. He kindled the hearts of the faithful; he gave the apostles an irresistible power to open a way for the Gospel. Only to them, finally, did he communicate himself in such fullness that they were able to communicate the gift to others by the laying-on of hands.

2. Apostolic succession is articulated on this precise point: just as Christ infused the Spirit in full and fruitful form, so necessarily did the apostles. The form is: assurance of the guidance of the Spirit in preaching the Word (*teacher*), share in the power of being a channel for the Gospel (*pastor*), and communication of the Spirit in his fruitful fullness, capable of begetting sons and even fathers for the Church (*pontifex*).

The beneficiaries of this infusion are the bishops, who occupy a place of preeminence in the Church, analogous to that held by the apostles in the beginning. Even though the Word is catholic and the Spirit knows no bounds, there are ministers specifically entrusted with preaching the Word and dispensing the Spirit, just as there were in the beginning. Derivation and posteriority (with the disappearance of those who went before) assure their succession.

Nothing could be harder than to explain the content of succession starting from the highly disputed concept of the bishop. Nothing, on the other hand, could be easier than to deduce the characteristics of a bishop starting from succession from the apostles.

IV

CONCLUSION

We have traced various developments which show stages of a notable progress:

1. Polemic gradually evolved into *dialogue*.
2. Apologists made common cause with *dogmatic* theologians.
3. Dogmatic theologians enlisted the help of *historians*.

How can progress be continued in the future? I think both the matter and the method of discussion need to be watched with great care: first, by purifying the spirit of *dialogue*, without shrinking from the extent of the problems fruitlessly jumbled together by polemicists; second, by centering the problem of apostolic succession on *ecclesiology*, to which it is genuinely barycentric, certainly, but without forgetting that ecclesiology in its turn hinges on *christology*, and that this leads in its turn to genuine *theology*. This is the only sure way to the heart of the mystery of the apostolic mission, bound up as it is with the two trinitarian mysteries.

Hans Küng/*Tübingen, W. Germany*

What Is the Essence of Apostolic Succession?

The concept of apostolic succession suffers from undue clerical and juridical constriction. We do not breathe the free air of the Bible and this paralyzes our ecumenism. New life can only be breathed into it by a return to Scripture. How this can be done is summarized here in a few theses with which I have dealt more in detail elsewhere.[1]

1. Basic is the point that the *whole Church* and *every individual member* share in this apostolic succession: the Church as a whole is committed to obedience to the apostles as the original witnesses and the original messengers. In the *negative* sense this means that the concept suffers from a clerical narrowing down if this apostolic succession is seen exclusively as a succession of ecclesiastical functions. In the *positive* sense it means that the whole Church is involved. It is the Church as a whole that we believe in when we say: "I believe in the apostolic Church." The Church as a whole is successor to the apostles. And insofar as the Church is not an institutional apparatus but the community of the faithful, this means that every individual member of the Church stands in this apostolic succession. Every later generation remains bound to the word, the witness and the service of the

---

[1] Cf. H. Küng, *Die Kirche, Ökumenische Forschungen*, I, 1 (Freiburg/Basle/Vienna, 1967), esp. Ch. D IV, 2; E II, 2.

first apostolic generation. The apostles are and remain the once-for-all and irreplaceable original witnesses: their witness, the sole original witness; their mission, the sole original mission. The whole Church is founded on the foundation of the apostles (and the prophets).

2. The apostolic succession of the Church as a whole and of every individual consists in this *essential cohesion with the apostles* to be put into practice constantly; it demands the constant accord with the apostolic *witness* (Scripture) and the constant rendering of the apostolic *service* (missionary extension in the world and the building up of the community). Apostolic succession is therefore primarily a succession in apostolic faith, apostolic service and apostolic life. This means in the *negative* sense that it is a juridical narrowing of the concept to see apostolic succession primarily in a continuous chain of impositions of hands—as if such a chain of ordinations by itself could supply the apostolic spirit! In the *positive* sense it means that the point of the succession lies in the constantly renewed daily loyalty to the apostles. This means, not fanaticism, but sober obedience. The apostles are dead. Any authority and power in the Church can only arise from obedience to the Lord of the Church and the apostles. Apostolicity is at the same time a gift and a task. Both the Church as a whole and every individual member need to be in harmony with the apostolic witness: they can only hear the Lord and his message *via* this apostolic witness. In fact, sound *ecclesiastical* tradition can only be an interpretation, explanation and application of the original *apostolic* tradition contained in Scripture. And the Church cannot be true to this apostolic witness otherwise than through continuing the apostolic service in its many forms of proclamation, baptism, the communion in prayer and the eucharistic meal, the building up of the community and service to the world.

3. Within the apostolic succession of the Church as a whole there is a special apostolic succession of the many *pastoral* services, through which the pastors, without being apostles themselves, continue the mission and function of the apostles, namely,

the founding and guiding of the Church. In the *negative* sense this means that apostolic succession becomes a mere abstraction if we divorce it from the historical reality. We must not only see the Church as a whole but also in the concrete reality of her many services which are not all equally important. In the *positive* sense it means that the pastors are not apostles but continue the mission and function of the apostles by founding and leading the Church. They are not a governing class with a one-sided power to command. But there is a superposition and a subordination determined by the kind of service.

4. Among the many charismatic gifts of leadership which continue the apostolic mission, the pastoral services of *presbyter* (pastor), *episkopos* (bishop) and *diakonos* (deacon), based on a particular function (imposition of hands), came to stand out with increasing prominence during the post-apostolic age. This means in the *negative* sense that we make an undue presupposition when we draw a simple straight line of succession from the apostles to the bishops. Apart from those charisms that appear freely and by their very nature cannot be brought under a system ("being the first", stewards, presidents, guides, etc.), it is equally impossible to systematize the services transmitted by imposition of hands (at least at that time) such as presbyters, *episkopoi,* deacons, etc., on the basis of the New Testament. The threefold order of functions mentioned by Ignatius of Antioch has, no doubt, its roots in the original period but cannot simply be identified as the whole original order and distribution of all the functions. It is the result of a very complex historical development. It is also impossible to trace the dividing line that separates these three functions among themselves, particularly in the case of the *episokopos* and the presbyter, on the basis of *dogmatic theology*. It means in the *positive* sense that the distinction between the various services is, on the one hand, a matter of factual development, and on the other, of pastoral expediency. Even if one wholly accepts the threefold division of the Church's function into presbyters, bishops and deacons as a meaningful and practical development, one cannot treat such a juridical definition,

which at most is the practical realization of *but one* possibility, as if it were a dogmatic necessity. The rich beginnings of a Church order in the New Testament leave plenty of room for other possibilities in practice.

5. Pastoral service as a special kind of succession to the apostles is surrounded in the Church by *other gifts* and services, particularly in those that have succeeded to the New Testament *prophets* and *teachers* who, in cooperation with the pastors, have their own original authority. This means in the *negative* sense that, through an unbiblical limitation, canalization and monopolization of the free charism in the Church, there arises a kind of pastoral hierocracy when pastors feel that they alone possess the Spirit and so try to quench the Spirit in others. There is an un-Pauline absolutization of a function when an official considers himself to be apostle, prophet and teacher all at once and so wants to grasp everything unto himself. In the *positive* sense it means that every individual stands in the line of apostolic succession according to the particular charism that has been bestowed on him. This succession is therefore not limited to the one line of pastoral services. There is also—and second in the order of St. Paul—the succession of the prophets in whom the Spirit expresses himself directly and who, in their awareness of their calling and responsibility, show the way, present and future, in a given situation of the Church. And, third in St. Paul's list, there is the succession of the teachers, the theologians who go to endless trouble in order to transmit and interpret in a genuine way the message of the past in the present situation of Church and world.

6. The *pastoral succession with imposition of hands* is neither automatic nor mechanical. It presupposes faith and demands a faith that is active in the apostolic spirit. It does not exclude the possibility of failure and error and therefore needs to be tested by the community of the faithful. This means in the *negative* sense: any isolated mechanism of succession of an official hierarchy which makes an abstraction of the human condition and, by the same token, of the constantly necessary grace of God and the

constantly new demands on faith and life, cannot appeal to the New Testament. The power of the community, of the universal priesthood, cannot be simply derived from the pastoral service. That would be an unbiblical clericalization of the community; it would separate the pastoral service from the universal priesthood and absolutize it in its succession. On the other hand, the power of the pastoral service also cannot be derived from the power of the community and the universal priesthood. This would be an unbiblical secularization of the community and reduce the pastoral function to the level of the universal priesthood. In the *positive* sense it means that cohesion *and* distinction of pastoral service and the community with all its special gifts and services are important. The special call to the *public service of the community as such* by the imposition of hands, the ordination, must be seen against the background of the universal priesthood. We must therefore distinguish between the "empowering" of every Christian and the special power of some individuals for the public service of the community as such. All Christians are empowered to proclaim the Word; to witness to the faith in the Church and in the world, all are "sent". But only those called to be pastors (or commissioned by them) have the special power to preach in the assembly of the community. All Christians are empowered to promise forgiveness to the brother troubled by conscience. But only those called to be pastors have the special power to pronounce the words of reconciliation and absolution in the assembly of the community as such and thus apply it to the individual. All Christians are empowered to take part in the administration of baptism and the eucharistic meal. But only those called to be pastors have the special power to administer baptism publicly and to preside responsibly over the communal eucharist.

7. The apostolic succession of the pastors must take place in the communion of mutual service to Church and world. Admission to the apostolic succession in the pastoral line should normally take place according to the mind of the New Testament through a *cooperation of pastors and community,* a cooperation of as many different elements as possible. This means in the

negative sense that it is a false view of ecclesiastical office to see obedience and subordination as a one-way traffic. The ecclesiastical functions are there for the community and not the community for the functions. An absolutist government of the Church, at the level of the whole Church, the diocese or the parish, is a contradiction of the Gospel. In the *positive* sense it means that, because of the specific mission of the pastor to the community, the pastoral function already implies an authority. The pastor has his credentials from the beginning and he is officially accepted as empowered to fulfill this public service for the community. Nevertheless, this in no way deprives the community of its right to examine whether the pastor acts in truth according to this mission, according to the Gospel. The specific power given to the pastor even requires that every day he obediently use this power anew. But in spite of all the legitimate relative autonomy of the pastor (bishop or priest) the appointment of pastors in the Church must come about basically through a cooperation of those who already are pastors and the community. And apart from their appointment, even when the pastors are entitled to a certain responsible autonomy in the guidance of the community because they need this in the exercise of their function, nevertheless, the community as the royal priesthood should have a voice in all the affairs of the community, and this can be done directly or through a representative body. This corresponds to the juridical principle, so often quoted in the Church's tradition: "What concerns all, must be dealt with by all."

8. If we base ourselves on the Pauline, or the Gentile Christian, Church order, we must leave room for *other ways of pastoral service and apostolic succession* of pastors. The Church order, based on the presbyter and the *episkopos,* which has as a matter of fact prevailed in the Church, must today, too, remain open in principle to all the possibilities that existed in the Church of the New Testament. This means in the *negative* sense that the institutional order, mainly determined by the Palestinian tradition must not be absolutized. The present organization of the

offices in the Church developed essentially in three stages: (a) over against the prophets, teachers and other charismatic functionaries, the episcopal line (including presbyters and *episkopoi*) prevailed as the dominant and finally exclusive leaders of the community; (b) over against the plurality of bishops (presbyters and bishops) within a community this led to a monarchical episcopacy; (c) from being the presidents of the individual communities the bishops became presidents of ecclesiastical territories.

This schematic sketch of the development cannot be ruled out *a priori* as unjustified. Nevertheless, a definite new order cannot be proved right simply by arguing from the existing situation nor from the possible misuse of charisms. It is justified rather by the decisive difference between the original phase and the time that came after, between the apostolic age of the foundation and the post-apostolic age of building up and expansion. In the *positive* sense this means: an exposé of the Pauline Church order can demonstrate that a charismatic order of the community is possible without a specific admission to a service (ordination), and that perchance Corinth knew of neither *episkopoi* nor presbyters nor any kind of ordination but only free and spontaneous charisms, apart from the apostles. And yet, according to Paul, the Church of Corinth was a community provided with all that was necessary, equipped with the proclamation of the Word, baptism, eucharist and all other services. On the other hand, there is at the same time enough evidence to show that these Pauline communities showed relatively soon that there were bishops and deacons, and, after Paul, ordained priests, so that the presbyteral and episcopal order became general in the Church. Nevertheless, the Church as she developed later cannot in principle exclude the Pauline Church order. However unlikely this order may be now, it can be important today for an extraordinary situation in the missions and particularly in the field of ecumenism.

And so my theses run into questions which need to be discussed, and today more urgently than ever before. Could the present Church wish or be able to prevent that somewhere—a concentration camp, distant captivity without contact with the outside, an extraordinary missionary situation (e.g. in Communist China, or in the case of those Japanese Christians who lived for centuries without ordained pastors)—the same thing should happen that happened in Corinth and other Pauline communities, namely, that guidance is simply provided by the free action of the Spirit of God through the charisms? When we assume the universal priesthood and the charismatic structure of the Church, should we still hold that the special apostolic succession via a series of impositions of hands is still the *only* and exclusive way into pastoral service, and should this be the only way in which we must think of apostolic succession? Even if this chain of impositions of hands is not taken so exclusively, would it still not remain an impressive sign of the apostolic succession in the pastoral line and therefore a sign of the unity, catholicity and apostolicity of the Church? Would we then not have every reason to judge apostolic succession and the validity of the eucharistic celebration in those Churches which are not part of this "chain" of ordinations in a different and much more positive manner? Would this not help us to see also other questions, like that of the ordination of women or that of Anglican orders, in a new light? And if we do not, is it at all possible to do justice to the full spiritual life, the fruitful activity of pastors, men and women, of other Churches? Is it then possible to mend the divisions of Christendom and to arrive at a mutual recognition? The enormous implications of these questions, both in theology and in the field of ecumenism, would seem obvious.

it. Over against the People of God stood this teaching, ruling Church. She no longer was regarded as the People of God itself, hierarchically structured and making its pilgrim way through the world".[8]

Limiting the notion of apostolic succession in the Church to succession within the hierarchy must derive from this same mentality: the Church (i.e. hierarchy) is set up over against the People of God. But apostolic succession within the hierarchy, which is meant to serve the People of God, can only be understood in relation to the apostolic succession of the whole Church. It is only because apostolic succession resides in the whole Church that it can be applied to the servant hierarchy.

In its *Constitution on the Church*, Vatican Council II introduces the term "succession" with regard to the heirs of the apostles' office in Chapter 3. Prior to this, however, in Chapter 2, it speaks of the People of God and the role of the Holy Spirit. He is "the fountainhead of unity and society for the whole Church and for each and every one of the faithful—in the teaching of the apostles and in fellowship, in prayer and the breaking of bread (cf. Acts 2, 42)" (n. 13). And the Church "has received this solemn command of Christ to proclaim the truth of salvation, and it must be carried to the ends of the earth" (n. 17).

When we talk about the apostolic succession of the "whole Church" here, we do not mean to set it up in opposition to "local Church". The two are distinct, but they are not to be set off against each other. We have several Russian Orthodox theologians (e.g., N. Afanassieff, A. Schmemann, J. Meyendorff, P. Evdokimov) to thank for the fact that the peculiar significance of the local Church has gained its rightful place once again.[9]

[8] Karl Rahner, "Die Sünde in der Kirche," in *De Ecclesia:* Commentaries on Vatican Council II's *Constitution on the Church,* edited by G. Baraúna (Freiburg-Frankfurt), I, p. 349.

[9] N. Afanassieff, N. Koulomizine, J. Meyendorff, A. Schmemann, *Primacy of Peter in the Orthodox Church* (New York, 1963); N. Afanassieff, "Le doctrine de la primauté à la lumière de l'ecclésiologie," in *Istina* (1957), pp. 401–20; "L'infaillibilité de l'Eglise du point de vue d'un théologien orthodoxe," in *L'Infaillibilité de l'Eglise* (Chevetogne, 1962), pp. 183–201; "Una Sancta," in *Irénikon* (1963), pp. 436–75; A.

Their "eucharistic ecclesiology" repeatedly emphasizes that the mystery of the Church becomes fully and truly operative in the communion banquet of the local Churches. The Church is not a sum total of local Churches; they are not parts of a larger whole. Local Churches make the Church present and real in a given place. In its unity with the local bishop and through its celebration of the Lord's eucharist, each local Church is the Church of God, enjoying the fullness of God's grace and bearing the notes of oneness, holiness, catholicity and apostolicity.

There may be no real opposition between "universal ecclesiology" and the "eucharistic ecclesiology" of these theologians. They probably complement and supplement one another. But the positive elements in the outlook of these theologians deserve much attention. In Scripture, too, we find that local Churches are called the Church of God (Acts 8, 1; 20, 17; Apoc. 2–3; 1 Cor. 10, 32; 15, 9; Gal. 1, 13; 1 Tim. 3, 5; 3, 15; Phil. 3, 6). Every local Church, like that in Judea, is the Church in Christ (Gal. 1, 22); it is linked to every place where people call upon the name of Jesus Christ (1 Cor. 1, 2).

I

THE APOSTLES AND APOSTOLIC SUCCESSION

As men who saw the risen Christ and who were the foundation

Schmemann, "Unity, Division, Reunion, in the Light of Orthodox Ecclesiology," *Theologia,* 22 (Athens, 1951), pp. 242ff; "Le Patriarche oecuménique et l'Eglise Orthodoxe," *Istina* (1954), pp. 30–45; J. Meyendorff, "Sacrement et hiérarchie dans l'Eglise: Contribution orthodoxe à un dialogue oecuménique sur la primauté romaine," in *Dieu Vivant,* 26 (1954), pp. 79–91; "Ecclesiastical Organization in the History of Orthodoxy," *St. Vladimir's Seminary Quarterly,* 4 (1960), pp. 2–22; *L'Eglise Orthodoxe hier et aujourd'hui* (Paris, 1960); cf. B. Schultze, "Eucharistie und Kirche in der russischen Theologie der Gegenwart," in *Zeitschr. f. Kath. Theologie,* 77 (1955), pp. 257–300; "Universal or Eucharistic Ecclesiology?" in *Unitas,* 17 (1965), pp. 87–106; E. Lanne, "Le mystère de l'Eglise dans la perspective de la théologie orthodoxe," in *Irénikon* (1962), pp. 171–212; Le Guillou, *Mission et Unité,* II pp. 195–99. H. J. Schultz, "The Dialogue with the Orthodox," in *Concilium,* Vol. 4 (1965), pp. 131–49; H. Marot, "Decrees of Vatican II: First Orthodox Reactions," *Concilium,* Vol. 14 (1966), pp. 134–54.

of the Church, the apostles were unique; no one could represent them or take their place.[10] In this sense there could be no successors and no apostolic succession. E. Schlink sees the dogmatic concept of "apostle" as composed of two essential elements: (1) eyewitness to the resurrection of Jesus Christ and (2) a mission given by the risen one.[11]

This conferral of a mission was also a fully empowered authorization. It was not an unrealizable demand, for it included a promise of divine fulfillment. It included a promise that Christ would be present and that the Spirit would be at work. Because of their unique position in history, their direct commission from the risen Christ, the apostles are the foundation of the Church—not just of individual communities but of the whole Church in all times and places (cf. Mt. 16, 18; Eph. 2, 20; Apoc. 21, 14).

With the death of the apostles, the apostolic office—characterized by the two notes listed above—could not go on. The mandate given to the apostles did not fade away, however, for it involves the evangelization of all peoples until the end of the world. Thus the mission of the apostles transcends their own person. It embraces the "all" over which Jesus has been placed as Lord—all peoples, all nations, all times right up to the Parousia.

As Schlink sees it, apostolic succession is not an attribute of the official hierarchy alone; it is also an attribute of the whole Church, deriving from the universal mission of all baptized people. It consists of these primary elements:

(a) Faith in the apostolic message and obedience to the apostles' exhortations and instructions.

(b) Bearing witness to the apostolic Gospel—a task entrusted to each and every Christian according to his individual charisms.

(c) Preaching to and winning over the world, and building up the community in the world. Every charism serves to

[10] H. Bacht, "Apostel," in *Lexicon für Theologie und Kirche* (Freiburg, 1957), I, p. 738.

[11] Edmund Schlink, "Die apostilische Sukzession," in *Der kommende Christus und die kirchlichen Traditionen* (Göttingen, 1961), pp. 160–95.

build up the community, and it operates in the realm where the Church and the world confront each other. In this sense, every Christian inherits the Church-building activity of the apostles and bears responsibility in their service as shepherds.

(d) Caring for the community with all Christians and all the Churches throughout the world. This is an essential aspect of the apostolic succession shared by the Church and by all Christians. Apostolic succession truly exists only insofar as the apostles are truly regarded as the bond of Church unity in all times and all places.[12]

The Catholic theologian will readily agree with Schlink on these points. There really is an apostolic succession enjoyed by the whole Church. Hans Küng puts it this way:

Who succeeds the apostles? There can be only one basic answer: the Church! It is not a few individuals but the whole Church which enjoys apostolic succession. We profess belief in the "apostolic Church".

The whole Church is the temple of the Holy Spirit built on the foundation of the apostles. The whole Church is the new People of God, gathered together by the apostles through their preaching of Christ's Gospel. The whole Church is the body of Christ, held together by the service of the apostles. Thus the authorized mission of the apostles has passed on to the Church which they gathered together, and their authorized service has passed over to the Church which they themselves served. The Church is the obedient successor of the apostles.

In obedience to this mission the Church acquires authority and power. It is on the basis of this apostolicity that she is truly one, holy and catholic. She must be grounded on the apostles. Thus it is not only an historical but also an objective succession; it involves an intrinsic, objective cohesion. This cohesion is not something provided by the Church alone; it is granted to her by the Spirit of God and Christ, it fills the apostles and their testimony, it stimulates and motivates the Church to imitation of them.[13]

---

[12] *Ibid.*, p. 192.
[13] Hans Küng, *Die Kirche,* Freiburg-Basel-Vienna, 1967, p. 421; cf. *Structures of the Church* (New York: Nelson, 1963).

II

APOSTOLIC SUCCESSION AND THE BELIEVING COMMUNITY

Since Pentecost, the Church has been an apostolic community of believers. To become a member of the Church means to be added (Acts 2, 41.47), to give increase (Acts 5, 14), to a community which is brought together by the word of the apostles; and their word is related to the Word of life. "Therefore, you are now no longer strangers and foreigners, but you are citizens with the saints and members of God's household: you are built upon the foundation of the apostles and prophets with Christ Jesus himself as the chief cornerstone. In him the whole structure is closely fitted together and grows into a temple holy in the Lord . . ." (Eph. 2, 19ff.).

The Church remains tied to her origins because our faith was delivered once for all (Jude 3). She remains subject to the norm of this origin because the "trans-historical seed" (P. Evdokimov[14] which was entrusted to the apostles has both an historical and an eschatological character. This seed is the Christ-happening itself, the saving action of God who "last of all in these days has spoken to us by his Son" (Heb. 1, 2). In the time-honored concept of *paradosis* (which is older than the concept of succession), the theme and concern was God's salvific plan; Jesus Christ was its meaning, its center, and its key figure.[15] Like the apostles, the Church is totally tied to his plan; her sole purpose is to carry on the service rendered by the apostles, to promote the reality of salvation by her obedience and self-sacrifice.

We become acquainted with the reality of Jesus Christ only through the witness of the apostles. Apostolic succession becomes operative in the ever new and living confrontation of the Church and all her members with the basic, pristine witness of the apostles; historically, this witness comes to the Church in the writings of the New Testament, which contain the Old Testament as

[14] P. Evdokimov, *L'Orthodoxie* (Neuchâtel-Paris, 1959), p. 161.
[15] Yves Congar, *La Tradition et les traditions* (Paris, 1960), I, p. 48 (Eng. tr.: *Tradition and Traditions in the Church*, New York: Macmillan, 1966).

well.[16] Here the New Testament is the message of salvation, the announcement of the basic, all-embracing reality of salvation promised in the Bible: our communion with God and our fellow men.

Apostolic witness is not primarily the communication of ideas and doctrines; it is the transmission of the Christ-happening, God's self-revelation through the words and deeds of Christ which form a unified whole.[17] This event establishes a personal salvation-community and invites us into it. Even after the apostles had died, tranmission of this revelation did not become the authoritative transmission of a doctrine. It remained the perduring and ever-present reality of this community fashioned by Christ; and this reality resides in the life of the Church as a whole. It is in this sense primarily that we can talk about the apostolic succession of the whole community of believers.

In discussing the Pre-Nicene Fathers, Congar makes some interesting observations.[18] In Irenaeus, for example, the notion of tradition as a formal doctrine appears within the general doctrine of apostolicity. Irenaeus, even more than the other Pre-Nicene Fathers, sees all of Christianity from the very beginning as the transmission and the unfolding of a single reality. Even as it spreads through time and space, it remains what it was from the very beginning; of its very nature it is apostolic. Christian communities received this tradition from the apostles, the apostles received it from Christ, and Christ received it from God.

The bearer of this tradition is the Church, the *ecclesia Dei*. Only she has received the apostolic deposit of truth, for only in her does the Holy Spirit dwell. Tradition must always be traced back to the apostles, its source, and to the Church, its bearer. The Church is, in the words of Cyprian, the *"plebs adunata sacerdoti et pastori suo grex adhaerens"* (*Epist.* 66.8.3). It is not an amorphous mass of loosely connected believers; it is a structured community with various services and offices. About 175 A.D.

---

[16] H. Küng, *Die Kirche*, p. 422.
[17] *Dogmatic Constitution on Divine Revelation*, n. 2.
[18] Yves Congar, *op. cit.*, p. 42f.

the notion of apostolic succession in the hierarchy[19] begins to be developed systematically, to counteract the Gnostic notion that tradition involves the oral communication of secret and mysterious doctrines; but this new development is tied up with the apostolicity of doctrine.

Legitimate succession in the hierarchy ensures and safeguards the apostolicity of Christian doctrine; it guarantees the authenticity of the tradition being handed down. But the bearer of this tradition is the whole Church, and the agreement of the whole community of believers is the proof and the criterion of its authenticity.

The Pentecost-event is the happening that fashions a community. The Holy Spirit comes down, not only on the apostles, but on all: "They were all filled with the Holy Spirit" (Acts 2, 4). This "all", of course, refers to all those who were praying in the upper room (Acts 1, 14). As Christ had promised (Jn. 7, 39), all who believed in him received the Spirit. Peter explained this event as the fulfillment of the prophecy made by Joel: "This is what was spoken by the prophet Joel, 'And it shall come to pass in the last days, says the Lord, that I will pour forth of my Spirit upon all flesh . . ." (Acts 2, 16–21; Joel 3, 1–5).

The enduring presence of the Holy Spirit in the community of believers is a touchstone of New Testament catechesis (Jn. 14, 16; Mk. 13, 11; Lk. 12, 12; Rom. 8, 9; 1 Cor. 3, 16). On the day that Jesus was baptized, the Spirit descended on Jesus to remain with him. So, too, the irrepeatable Pentecost-happening—the descent of the Spirit upon the Church—has perduring significance; it establishes the immortality of the Church, it makes her "the pillar and mainstay of the truth" (1 Tim. 3, 15).

There was still another communication of the Spirit, as John 20, 22–23 tells us. When the apostles were huddled in the room where they had eaten the last supper, the risen Christ breathed the Holy Spirit into them; thus the officials in the Church bear

---

[19] C. H. Turner, "Apostolic Succession," in *Essays on the Early History of the Church and the Ministry,* edited by H. B. Swete (London, 1921), pp. 95–214.

the Spirit in a very special way and have the distinctive duty of leading the Church (Acts 20, 28); but they have no monopoly on the Spirit, and they cannot act as if they alone were the Church. The Holy Spirit dwells in all the baptized.[20]

Here we must stress an important point. It cannot be claimed that the presence of the Spirit of Truth in the Church comes about through the mediation of the hierarchy. As J. C. Groot has pointed out recently: "To be sure, the mediation of the hierarchical office has played an important role from the very beginning in the building up of the Church. It has also rendered its share of service in the communication of the Spirit. But insofar as we are talking about the Church as the community of believers, as a "communion", we cannot say that the sending of the Spirit has come about through the mediation of the hierarchy. In the Church as "communio", the presence of the Spirit is the fruit of a direct, immediate sending as happened at Pentecost." [21]

We can say that the Church, as the communion of believers, is the pillar and ground of truth itself, that is, by virtue of the Pentecost Spirit who resides in her. The believing, loving Church as such is animated by the Holy Spirit; through this animation she is infallible and has an organic relationship vis-à-vis the hierarchy. The universal priesthood of the faithful and their participation in Christ's prophetic office have their peculiar significance in view of the apostolic succession of the whole Church.

There is only one priest, teacher and shepherd present and working through the Spirit in the Church and all her members, operating through the special service of the hierarchy for the good of his Church. The Church as a whole, therefore, does not have a secondary, passive share in the gift of infallibility—simply obeying what she hears from the hierarchy.[22] This view hardly accords with Vatican Council II's statements on the Church

[20] Jean Jacques von Allmen, "L'Esprit de vérité vous conduira dans toute la vérité," in L'Infaillibilité de l'Eglise, pp. 13–26.

[21] J. C. Groot, "Die horizontalen Aspekte der Kollegialität," in De Ecclesia (edited by G. Baraúna) II, p. 86.

[22] B. van Leeuwen, "Die allgemeine Teilnahme am Prophetenamt Christi," ibid., I, pp. 393–419.

body's understanding of the faith: "The universal body of the faithful, who have the Holy One's anointing (1 Jn. 2, 20.27) cannot err in belief" (*Constitution on the Church,* n. 12).

This infallibility is based on the supernatural understanding of the whole body, on the universal mission of the Spirit of Truth and on the Spirit's anointing. "Through this discernment the People of God . . . with sound judgment penetrates deeper into this faith, and applies it more fully in actual life" (*ibid.*). Although the infallible teaching and guidance of the official magisterium is included here too, one cannot make the *consensus fidelium* entirely dependent on the teaching activity of the hierarchy. To do this would be to contradict the primacy and the normative character of the Church community as a whole. To do this would be to make light of the fact that the Spirit of Pentecost entered the Church, the bride of Christ, without the mediation of the hierarchy; and that it continues to maintain the believing community's attachment to Christ and the apostle in Word and sacrament.[23]

III

THE CONTINUING APOSTOLIC MISSION

"At bottom the apostolicity of the Church maintains the identity of mission between the present-day Church and the apostles and, *mutatis mutandis,* between the apostles and Christ, the first 'envoy' of God." [24] In this sense, the apostolic succession of the Church can be viewed as a process of succession in the mission that lies at the core of the Church. This is so because the Church has received from the apostles Christ's mandate to preach the truth of salvation (Acts 1, 8); but that is not the only reason. Even more importantly, this mandate is an arrangement that corresponds to the ontological-sacramental structure of the People of God and actually presupposes this structure. This sacramental

[23] Cf. J. C. Groot, *op. cit.,* p. 95.
[24] Yves Congar, "Apostolicité," in *Catholicisme,* 1 (Paris, 1948), p. 729.

structure[25] must here be understood in terms of the ancient expressions *mysterion* and *sacramentum,* as they applied to the Christian salvation-reality and, most importantly of all, to Christ himself: he himself is the embodiment of God's eternal plan, the actualization of it and the revelation of it (Rom. 16, 25–26; Eph. 1, 9–14; 3, 3–4 and 8–9; Col. 1, 26–27; 2, 2).

Christ is *the* sacrament, the proto-sacrament, because in him God's salvific plan takes concrete form and becomes a reality on this earth; he is to subject all things to himself, until God becomes all in all (1 Cor. 15, 28). The sacramental character of the Church rests on this proto-sacrament. As the *Constitution on the Church* points out: "The Church exists in Christ as a sacrament or sign and an instrument of intimate union with God and of the unity of the whole human race" (n. 1). And as Vatican Council II's *Decree on the Missionary Activity of the Church* says, the Church is "the universal sacrament of salvation" (n. 1).

Obviously, these texts are referring to the Church as the whole People of God and ascribing a sacramental character to it. She is a sign that betokens a reality because in her the God of salvation is revealed among men and his plan is effectively realized. She is an "instrument of salvation", but an instrument that sticks close to the Spirit of the redeemer even as his humanity adheres to his divine person.

P. Smulders[26] has spelled out more clearly what the *Constitution on the Church* means when it calls the Church a sacrament, a sign and instrument. The Church is not simply an instrument

---

[25] O. Semmelroth, *Die Kirche als Ursakrament* (Frankfurt, 1953); "Um die Einheit des Kirchenbegriffs," in *Fragen der Theologie heute* (Einsiedeln 1957), pp. 319–35. K. Rahner, *Church and the Sacraments* (New York: Herder and Herder, 1963); E. Schillebeeckx, *Christ: The Sacrament of the Encounter with God,* trans. New York: Sheed and Ward. P. Smulders, "Die Kirche as Sakrament des Heils," in *De Ecclesia* (edited by Baraúna) *op. cit.,* I, pp. 289–312; G. Bornkamm, "Mustèrion," in *Th. W.N.T.,* 4 (Kittel, 1942), pp. 809–34; E. Schillebeeckx, *De sacramentele Heilseconomie* (Antwerp-Bilthoven, 1952); C. Mohrmann, "Sacramentum dans les plus anciens textes chrétiens," in *Harvard Theological Review,* 47 (1954), pp. 40–152.

[26] P. Smulders, "Die Kirche als Sakrament des Heils," in *De Ecclesia* (edited by Baraúna) *op. cit.,* pp. 306–07.

or a servant. She is, in a way, the salvation that has been effected, the new creation shaped in the image of its creator that has been brought about. She puts on the definitive unity of God's chosen people, and thus she serves the unity she is trying to fashion. She is the earthly face of salvation, the pre-fulfillment and the seed of God's ultimate and definitive dominion over the earth. She is the sign and instrument of salvation because she is the firstfruits of salvation.

Through Christ's commission to his apostles, the apostolic mission of the Church rests on the sacramental structure of the People of God as a whole. The priestly, prophetic and kingly People of God has been commissioned by Christ to unite all mankind and the whole world. It is to fulfill God's will, to "gather into one the children of God who were scattered abroad" (Jn. 11, 52) and "to re-establish all things in Christ, both those in the heavens and those on the earth" (Eph. 1, 9–10).

Not only by virtue of her catholicity (which the *Constitution on the Church,* n. 13, stresses), but also by virtue of the gift of apostolicity God has conferred on her, the Church receives and preserves the *pleroma* of Christ—not as a static inheritance but as a mission of service. By her very structure the Church is obligated to be apostolic. The sacramental mystery of the Church obliges her to carry on unceasingly her original mission, to serve as an instrument of salvation for the world in history and society. She does this primarily through preaching and the eucharist, trying to bring to mankind the fullness of unity and brotherhood which the eucharist promises and provides.

In connection with the laity, Vatican Council II stresses the fact that there is only one mission and one apostolate. In its *Decree on the Apostolate of the Laity,* it points out: "In the Church herself there is a unity of mission but many kinds of ministry . . . Lay people have also been made sharers in the priestly, prophetic and royal office of Christ, and thus they exercise their proper role in the mission of the whole People of God, both within the Church and in the secular order" (n. 2).

"The place of lay Christians in the mission of the Church is an integral and altogether essential one. Their apostolate flows from the very calling to be followers of Christ . . ." (n. 1). For more than a century and a half, this principle was unheard of in the Catholic Church.[27] Pius IX never said a word about it. Pius XII mentioned it only with the greatest caution.

This principle makes any special treatment regarding the lay apostolate a very delicate undertaking. There is no separation between the lay apostolate and that of the priests and the hierarchy; for all are called to the same apostolate by virtue of the fact that they are Christians. "Lay people have a right and duty to exercise the apostolate which stems from their very union with Christ the Head. By baptism they are joined to the mystical body of Christ; they are strengthened by the power of the Holy Spirit in confirmation; and they are thus commissioned to the apostolate by the Lord himself" (ibid., n. 3).

A basic outlook on Christianity took shape during Vatican Council II, some insights flashing suddenly to light, others taking much time and trouble. This basic outlook was that the community of believers as a whole, not the hierarchy or the ecclesiastical leadership, should have the primary place.[28] We may happily regard this as a rediscovery of the biblical notion that the Church is an *adelphotes,* a brotherhood of believers; it is a much broader and deeper notion than the juridical concept of *collegium.*[29]

In Chapter 4 of the *Constitution on the Church,* Vatican Council II notes that "the holy Church, of divine institution, is ordered and governed with wondrous diversity". At the same time, however, it goes on to stress the equality and the oneness of God's People with particular emphasis: "Thus there is one

[27] A. C. Ramselaar, "Het Conciliedecreet over het Lekenapostolaat," in *Theologie en Zielzorg* (1966), pp. 233–57, esp. p. 245.

[28] B. A. Willems, "Kerkelijke gemeenschap en kerkelijke leiding in de conciliekonstitutie over de Kerk," in *Tijdschrift voor theologie,* 6 (1966), pp. 51–159.

[29] Cf. J. Ratzinger, "The Pastoral Implications of Episcopal Collegiality," *Concilium* 1 (1965), pp. 39–67.

chosen People of God, 'one Lord, one faith, one baptism' (Eph. 4, 5); the members share a common dignity from their regeneration in Christ, a common grace of sonship, a common vocation to perfection, one salvation, one hope, and one undivided charity" (n. 32).

The apostolic mission of the Church is fulfilled, in all its essentials, in the Twelve. Thus the mission of the faithful makes them co-workers with the apostles, participants in their mission and imitators of their deeds. Even though all are equal by virtue of their unity in the Spirit, this does not mean that they have equal duties and services to perform. The People of God, to which the laity and the clergy belong, is neither lay nor clerical itself. The clerical and lay elements in the People of God represent different types of *diakonia,* different types of service. The Spirit operates through the interplay of varied gifts, charisms and abilities (cf. Rom. 12, 3ff.; 1 Cor. 12, 4ff.). Thus, in accordance with God's will, some are appointed teachers, dispensers of the mysteries of God and shepherds for the sake of others.

The apostolic succession of the hierarchy operates within the apostolic succession of the whole believing community. In their witness, which is grounded on the witness of Christ and the apostles, the hierarchy is surrounded by the witness of all those who have received the Spirit. The Pentecost-event leaves room for the service of both the hierarchy and the believing community; by virtue of this perduring Spirit of Pentecost, the risen Lord weaves total harmony between the preaching, teaching and sanctifying of the hierarchy and the faith-inspired witness of his priestly People.

The hierarchy must do what the apostles did. They must work for the community, united with the other members of the Church and with the services that have been entrusted to the latter. In their apostolic succession, "the hierarchy never stands apart from their communities; following in the footsteps of the apostles, they come to their communities with a dire need for the intercession and the cooperation of the royal priesthood of all the faithful, with a dire need for the charisms of the latter. All these things express the apostolic succession that belongs to the whole Church and to all her members".[30]

After noting that the apostolic succession of the hierarchy "cannot be isolated from the total reality transmitted, the Church herself", Congar goes on to make this point: "Buried in the reality of apostolic succession is the principle of *sobornost* ('collegiality'). It suggests that there is some type of control exercised by the whole Church, some scheme of 'reception'. There is abundant testimony to these realities in history, but they got lost in professional theology through an overemphasis on the juridical aspect of things." [31]

Renewed consideration of the hierarchy as a service to the community, within a theology of the Church as a Communion, seems to offer us a great change to overcome this "juridicism".[32] Within this perspective, it seems, treatment of the apostolic succession of the whole community should be given precedence over treatment of hierarchical succession.

[30] H. Küng, *Strukturen der Kirche,* p. 169 (Eng. tr.: *Structures of the Church,* New York: Nelson, 1963).

[31] Yves Congar, "Apostolicité de ministère et apostolicité de doctrine," *op. cit.,* pp. 107–08.

[32] K. H. Schelkle, *Jüngerschaft und Apostelamt* (Freiburg, 1961); O. Semmelroth, *Das geistliche Amt* (Frankfurt, 1958); Yves Congar, "La hierarchie comme service selon le Nouveau Testament et les documents de la Tradition," in *L'Episcopat et l'Eglise universelle* (Paris, 1962), pp. 67–99; H. Küng, *Strukturen der Kirche,* pp. 166ff. (Eng. tr.: *op. cit.*); *Die Kirche,* pp. 458ff.

Avery Dulles, S.J./*Woodstock, Md.*

The Succession of Prophets in the Church

In the primitive Church the ministry of the Word was exercised by different classes of persons, including apostles, evangelists, teachers and various charismatic figures. Among the charismatics the place of highest dignity belonged to the prophets (1 Cor. 14, 1), who are regularly ranked second after the apostles, and thus above the teachers (1 Cor. 12, 28; Eph. 2, 20; 3, 5; 4, 11). If the Church of today is the continuation of the apostolic Church, one might expect to find in her persons having the same or equivalent gifts. That bishops are successors to the apostles has long been an accepted Catholic thesis. But have we sufficiently attended to the problem: Who, if anyone, has taken over the functions of the prophets and teachers?

The problem of succession in the prophetic line seems to offer special difficulty, since prophecy is by its nature a charismatic gift, distributed by the Holy Spirit when and as he wills. Yet it seems clear that charismatic gifts have not died out in the Church. Up to most recent times, visionaries and ecstatics have made their appearance, and there have been periodic outbursts of glossalalia resembling the biblical "gift of tongues". As the magisterium itself teaches, the completeness of the Church in every age demands both hierarchical grades and charismatic gifts, so that charismatically endowed persons will never be wanting to the

Church.[1] Thus we ought to consider seriously whether there are not, or should not be, successors of the prophets in the contemporary Church.

I

PROPHETS IN THE CHURCH

According to Acts (2, 16f.) St. Peter interpreted the miracle of Pentecost as evidence that the whole Church was a prophetic community, animated by the Holy Spirit. God had fulfilled Joel's oracle, "Your sons and your daughters shall prophesy." But from the New Testament as a whole it is clear that certain individuals were specially called to exercise the prophetic ministry (Rom. 12, 6; 1 Cor. 12, 6–10. 28–29).[2] While these prophets were in some cases itinerant preachers (e.g., Judas Barsabbas, Silas, Agabus), the majority seem to have been leading figures in the local communities. According as the Spirit gave them, they would utter words of praise or condemnation; they would summon to penance or to renewed hope. The effects of prophecy are described as edification, encouragement and consolation (1 Cor. 14, 3).

For the sake of accuracy, one must distinguish the prophets from the apostles, evangelists, teachers and ecstatics. They differ from apostles in that they do not speak as official witnesses of the risen Christ, but give more particular admonitions on the basis of what the Spirit teaches them. Unlike evangelists, they are not missionaries; they proclaim not the basic news of God's salvific deed in Christ but its further implications for life and conduct. Thus they speak within the Christian community. They differ also from teachers, since they are concerned not with gen-

[1] *Mystici Corporis* n. 17. *Acta Apost. Sedis* (1943), 200.

[2] On the New Testament prophets one may consult G. Friedrich, "Prophētēs (N.T.)," in *Theol. Wörterb. z. N. T.* VI, pp. 829–863; P. Vielhauer, "Propheten im Christentum (im N.T.)," in *Rel. in Gesch. und Gegenw.*[3] V. pp. 633f.

eral points of doctrine but with urging, on the basis of an inspired insight, the course to be taken in the present concrete situation. In connection with their admonitions the prophets not infrequently predict things to come, especially in the proximate future (e.g., Acts 11, 28; 21, 9f.). They differ, finally, from the ecstatics, because they are not rapt out of their senses. They speak with full self-possession in a language that all can understand (1 Cor. 14, 6–25).

Although the author of the Apocalypse, imitating the style of some Old Testament prophets, claims unquestionable authority for his message (Apoc. 22, 18f.), the majority of the New Testament prophets are considered to be subject to critical scrutiny. Their message is to be rejected if it contradicts the Church's christological faith (1 Cor. 12, 3; 1 Jn. 4, 2) or fails to harmonize with orthodox teaching (Rom. 12, 6, according to one interpretation). But these doctrinal tests, valid though they may be, are insufficient. Even miracles are not a sure criterion, for false prophets are able to deceive by signs and wonders (cf. Mk. 13, 22ff.). The good or evil fruits of the prophet's teaching are another sign (Mt. 7, 15–23). But the final assessment requires prudence and insight. The gift of discernment is itself a special charism (cf. 1 Cor. 12, 10). The entire community should normally play a part in the process of discernment (1 Cor. 14, 29–33; cf. 1 Thess. 5, 21; 1 Jn. 4, 1).

II

OPPOSITION BETWEEN PROPHETISM AND SACERDOTALISM

The Fathers of the first two centuries took it for granted that the charism of prophecy was a permanent endowment of the Church. In the *Didache* (nn. 11–13) elaborate rules are laid down for the reception of visiting prophets and for distinguishing genuine prophets from their counterfeits. Some have seen in these prescriptions an indication that certain communities, having no prophets of their own, had to depend on visitors to fill their role.

About the middle of the 2nd century, Justin argues in his *Dialogue with Trypho the Jew* that "from the fact that even to this day the gifts of prophecy exist among us Christians, you should realize that the gifts which resided among your people have now been transferred to us".[3] Miltiades, who was probably a pupil of Justin, was heavily engaged in the struggle against Montanism. He set it down as a rule that a true prophet does not speak in ecstasy.[4] Notwithstanding the aberrations of the Montanists, Miltiades is convinced that, according to the doctrine of St. Paul, "it is necessary that the charism of prophecy should be present in the whole Church until the final parousia".[5] Irenaeus, who was likewise concerned with the growing combat with false prophets, felt it necessary to defend true prophecy. Some, he observed, in their excess of zeal against the pseudo-prophets, go so far as to reject the grace of genuine prophecy in the Church.[6]

By the 3rd century charismatic prophecy begins to be viewed as a thing of the past. Origen in his controversies with Celsus so treats it.[7] As the Church becomes increasingly a society of law and doctrine, the magisterium and theologians gain fuller control of the ministry of the Word. This trend continued in the Middle Ages, when prophecy fared best in what Knox calls the Christian underworld.

St. Thomas, from his intellectualist point of view, is concerned with prophecy as a supernatural mode of knowledge. It interests him principally as a means by which the deposit of faith was built up in biblical times. At the end of his treatise on prophecy he adds, almost by way of concession, that even after apostolic

[3] *Dial.* n. 82. Transl. T. B. Falls, in *Fathers of the Church* (New York, 1948), p. 278.

[4] As quoted in Eusebius, *Hist. Eccl.* V, 17, 1. Coll. *Sources chrét.* 41 (Paris, 1955), p. 53.

[5] *Ibid.*, 17, 4; *Sources chrét.*, 54. It is not clear what Pauline texts Miltiades had in mind. G. Bardy, in the *Sources chrét.* edition, suggests 1 Cor. 1, 7 taken in combination with Eph. 4, 11. E. Fascher, "Propheten (in der altchristlichen Kirche)," in *Rel. in Gesch. und Gegenw.*[3] V, p. 635, accepts this suggestion. R. Knox, *Enthusiasm* (Oxford, 1950), pp. 43f. refers to 1 Cor. 13 as a possible source.

[6] *Adv. Haer.* III.11.9. *Sources chrét.* 34 (Paris, 1952), pp. 203–205.

[7] *Contra Celsum* VII.11. *P.G.* 11:1456–57.

times "there were not lacking some endowed with a spirit of prophecy, not indeed for declaring any new teaching of faith, but for the direction of human actions".[8] While acknowledging that post-biblical prophets may be useful insofar as they serve to correct men's behavior, he seems to give them no role in casting light on what people should believe.[9] For the lacunae in St. Thomas' doctrine of prophecy one may assign three main factors, all rooted in the mental climate of his day: a sharp dichotomy between the speculative and practical intellect, the lack of any realization of the importance of post-biblical history,[10] and a spirituality intensely focused on man's hope for eternal life hereafter.

As the mere mention of Bernard of Clairvaux, Francis of Assisi and Catherine of Siena should suffice to prove, prophetism remained in lively tension with sacerdotalism throughout the Middle Ages. But the frequency with which prophetic spirits in the later Middle Ages ended up as heretics or martyrs (St. Joan, Savonarola) seems to indicate that the institutional Church was becoming less receptive to prophetic criticism. Several Catholic ecclesiologists have seen the ecumenical significance of this development. The history of the Reformation might have been quite different if the Church in the 16th century had been more open to searching scrutiny in the light of the Gospel.[11] In post-Reformation times, the history of Western Christianity is dominated by the struggle between the prophetism of the Reformation

---

[8] *Summa theol.* IIa–IIae, q. 174, a. 6, ad 3.

[9] Cf. S. Thomas, *Comment. in Matth.* xi.1. For commentary see C. Journet, *The Church of the Word Incarnate* 1 (London, 1955), p. 137, note 2 (French orig., *L'Eglise du Verbe Incarné* 1 [Bruges, 1941]); also L. Volken, *Visions, Revelations and the Church* (New York, 1963), pp. 221–225 (French orig., *Les révélations dans l'Eglise* [Mulhouse, 1961]).

[10] On St. Thomas's theology of history, as contrasted with that of Bonaventure and other contemporaries, see Y. Congar, "Le sens de 'l'économie' salutaire dans la 'théologie' de S. Thomas d'Aquin," in *Glaube und Geschichte* (Festgabe J. Lortz II) (Baden-Baden, 1958), pp. 73–122.

[11] Cf. Y. Congar, *Vraie et fausse Réforme dans l'Eglise* (Paris, 1950), pp. 198–200; H. Küng, *The Council, Reform and Reunion* (New York, 1961), p. 73 (German orig., *Konzil und Wiedervereinigung* [Freiburg i. Br. ³1961]).

Churches and the sacerdotalism of the Catholic tradition. In a separation that ought never to have occurred, Churches of the Word were arrayed against Churches of the sacrament. From the standpoint of Russian Orthodoxy, Solovyev and Berdyaev added their own prophetic protest against the priestly bent of Roman Catholicism. "More than all other Christianities," writes Knox, "the Catholic Church is institutional." [12]

In Catholic theological literature since the Reformation, prophecy was progressively demoted to the point where it became regarded primarily as an extrinsic sign validating the authority of persons claiming to speak in the name of God. In this view, the content of prophecy was deprived of intrinsic interest. In order to achieve its purposes, prophecy had to be a prediction of verifiable historical occurrences. Little attention was paid to prophecy in the traditional sense of a disclosure of God's plans and purposes in history.

A certain renewal in the theology of prophecy began with the deeper study of ecclesiology in the past century. But Catholic authors, defensively oriented against Protestant positions, were reluctant to admit any real friction between the prophets and the magisterium. Many on the contrary took the view that prophecy was nothing more than the discharge of what they called the "prophetic office" of the Church—an office identified, for all practical purposes, with the magisterium.

There is a profound sense in which the Church has succeeded to the prophetic role of Christ and has become, in Newman's phrase, "God's prophet or messenger" in the world. As Newman goes on to explain, a prophet

is one who comes from God, who speaks with authority, who is ever one and the same, who is precise and decisive in his statements, who is equal to successive difficulties, and can smite or overthrow error. Such has the Catholic Church shown herself in her history, and such is she at this day. She

[12] Knox, *Enthusiasm*, p. 590. But as Knox also points out, normative Protestantism had its own conflicts with the "prophets of Zwickau" and the radical wing of the Reformation.

alone has the divine spell of controlling the reason of man, and of eliciting faith in her word from high and low, educated and ignorant, restless and dull-minded.[13]

Newman the convert and archenemy of Liberalism might well be impressed by these aspects of the Church. But one may question whether his view does justice to the full biblical concept of prophecy, especially as we find it in the Church of the New Testament. From the standpoint of the 20th century, moreover, Newman's ecclesiology seems excessively monolithic and triumphal.

III

THE PROPHETS ACCORDING TO VATICAN COUNCIL II

The *Constitution on the Church* of Vatican II, in an idiom more congenial to our times, teaches in its second chapter that the Church as a whole has a prophetic function (n. 12). Chapters 3 and 4 go on to explain how the prophetic office is exercised both through the authoritative teaching of the hierarchy (n. 25) and through the unofficial witness of the laity (n. 31). Christ, we are told, fulfills his prophetic office through the laity insofar as he "made them his witnesses and gave them understanding of the faith and the grace of speech (cf. Acts 2, 17–18; Apoc. 19, 10), so that the power of the Gospel might shine forth in their daily social and family life" (n. 35). But in spite of the biblical allusions, the conception of prophecy here advanced seems to be only a pale reflection of the charism described in the New Testament. The discussion of charisms in chapter 1 (n. 7) makes no special mention of prophecy. Nor does the *Decree on the Apostolate of the Laity,* in its treatment of the layman's "prophetic role", come any closer to the biblical conception outlined above.

The Council's principal contribution toward a renewal of the

---

[13] *Discourses to Mixed Congregations* (London, [7]1886), p. 279.

theology of prophecy is to be found in passages other than those that deal expressly with the charisms and the prophetic office. The *Decree on Ecumenism* and the *Pastoral Constitution on the Church in the Modern World* have far-reaching implications in this regard.

The *Decree on Ecumenism,* without expressly mentioning the gift of prophecy, makes ample room for prophetic criticism of the Church by those inside and outside her membership. It calls attention to the urgent need for Catholics to "make an honest and careful appraisal of whatever needs to be renewed and achieved in the Catholic household itself" (n. 4). A little later (n. 6) it declares that "Christ summons the Church, as she goes on her pilgrim way, to that continual reformation of which she always has need, insofar as she is an institution of men here on earth". In the following paragraph (n. 7) the Decree embodies a humble confession of sins against unity. All this contrasts strikingly with the previous tendency of Catholics to justify all the ways of their own Church and to dismiss ecclesiastical reformation as a Protestant preoccupation.

The *Constitution on the Church in the Modern World* deals in a genuinely prophetic spirit with the task of "scrutinizing the signs of the times and of interpreting them in the light of the Gospel" (n. 4). In a crucial topic sentence the Constitution goes on to state the presuppositions of prophetic activity, especially the twofold confidence that the Church is led by the Spirit of God and that God manifests his presence and purposes in events of the present age (n. 11). Recognizing the complexity of contemporary developments, the Church freely confesses that she does not always have at hand a solution to particular problems (n. 33) but feels the need of "special help, particularly in our day, when things are changing very rapidly and the ways of thinking are exceedingly various" (n. 44). Only through the assistance of all who may be favored with light and understanding can the Church hope successfully to "hear, distinguish and interpret the many voices of our age and to judge them in the light of the divine Word" (*ibid.*).

IV

PROPHETS IN THE CHURCH TODAY

Through documents such as those just mentioned, Vatican Council II expressed the need for prophetic guidance. The demand is not for ecstatics caught up into another world but for men capable of discerning God's hand in the history of our times. Prophecy in this sense must, in Rahner's words, "contain concrete and timely imperatives for our day, deriving from the general theology of the future and of history which Scripture already gives us." [14] The Israelite prophets of the classical period spoke in this way. Even in their predictions they did not appeal to clairvoyance. "The contents of these predictions are always related to contemporary historical circumstances and may be explained as the result of a normal faculty of observation combined with an intensified insight into the religious and moral situation of Israel." [15] Conscious of the new and urgent demands of God's Word, they castigated the deficiencies of a religion which was in danger of formalism and superstition. They issued a ringing challenge to repentance and reform.

The current demand for prophets in the Church is due in part to the revolutionary changes in our time. Under pain of irrelevance the Church can no longer ignore the course of world history. The rapidly evolving secular culture of our day puts questions to the Church for which there are no ready-made solutions. Scrutinizing the signs of the times, Christianity must reinterpret its own doctrine and goals in relation to the world of today. To effect this transposition without loss of substance is a task calling for prophetic insight.

Churchmen are always tempted to suppress prophecy, for it is a disturbing element. By upsetting men's settled views and destroying their complacencies, it continually threatens the unity

---

[14] K. Rahner, *Visions and Prophecies* (Quaestiones Disputatae 10) (New York, 1963), p. 106 (German orig., *Visionen und Prophezeiungen,* Freiburg i. Br., ²1958).

[15] J. Lindblom, *Prophecy in Ancient Israel* (Oxford, 1962), p. 199.

and stability of the institutional Church. Yet the Church needs prophecy. "A Church in which the prophets had to remain silent would degenerate into a spiritless organization" and its pastors would become mere bureaucrats.[16] In such a Church men would be suffocated by the fumes of a decaying sacerdotalism. As George Bernard Shaw once declared, a fruitful tension must be maintained among the regal, sacerdotal and prophetic powers. "We must accept the tension and maintain it nobly without letting ourselves be tempted to relieve it by burning the thread." [17]

St. Paul exhorted his communities to have deep respect for prophecy (1 Thess. 5, 20) and to aspire after prophetic gifts (1 Cor. 14, 1. 39). Subsequent history has shown that when prophets are not given their say within the Church, they rise up to condemn her from outside. Vatican Council II therefore acted wisely in exposing the Church to harsh winds of prophetic criticism from within her own ranks.

If the priest needs the prophet, the reverse is also true. A Church governed by prophets alone would be no better than one without prophets. When the ostensible prophets disagree, others must mediate between them. When they go beyond the bounds of practicality, as prophets are wont to do, others must stress the values of moderation, compromise and civility.

The two gifts of priesthood and prophecy, far from being antithetical, require each other. At times they are even found in the same individual. Several of Israel's greatest prophets, including Ezekiel, were priests. Christ himself, the eschatological prophet *par excellence,* is the eternal high priest. And in our own time, the most truly prophetic figure in the Church, John XXIII, was a pope. The prophetic priest is sometimes torn by painful conflict between loyalty to the institution which he serves and discontent with its present condition. But is this not the inescapable fate of one who accepts a ministry in the Church which was born on Pentecost? While working within the institutional framework to

16 H. Küng, *Die Kirche* (Freiburg i. Br., 1967), p. 510.
17 *Saint Joan* (New York, 1924), Preface, lv.

which he owes his message and his forum, the priest must be conscious of the defects and limitations of institutional religion. Otherwise he would turn into a mere functionary.

If the prophet and the priest are not one and the same person, let them at least, like Moses and Aaron, be brothers. For their ultimate goals are the same. The prophet, unless he is to undermine the basis of his own protest, must stand in solidarity with the Church. And his goal must ultimately be constructive. Since all the gifts of the Spirit are bestowed "for building up the body of Christ" (Eph. 4, 11), the prophet as well as the priest must "strive to excel in building up the Church" (1 Cor. 14, 12).

Arnold van Ruler / *Utrecht, Netherlands*

Is There a "Succession of Teachers"?

I

THE MANY WAYS OF SERVING THE TRUTH

Two things strike us in the New Testament. The first is that, from the beginning and in all kinds of connections, there is talk of doctrine, teaching and teachers. The second is that in such an important passage as 1 Corinthians 12, 28f. the teachers (*didaskaloi*) are named with the prophets immediately after the apostles, apparently long before *episkopoi* and presbyters.

In the New Testament and early Christianity these teachers show a remarkable flexibility and variety. Scholars are still baffled by a great number of questions, of which I shall only mention the most important. The teaching function, like every other one in the community, naturally had a "pneumatic" (spiritual, as dependent on the Spirit) character. But did this imply ecstasy or even only enthusiasm? Was teaching a purely momentary charismatic action of any member of the community? Or were there already, apart from these members, teachers that were appointed, possibly from among the presbyters? Were they peripatetic, going from place to place, or were they tied to a specific community? Was the idea mainly that they engaged in missionary activity among the pagans or that they were obliged to contribute pastorally to the building up of existing communities?

There is also much difference of opinion about the content of their teaching. Did they treat the Old Testament as was the custom in the synagogue? Did they read the Old Testament in the new light of the Spirit? Or did they work mainly at trying to prove the messianic character of Jesus from the Old Testament? Was it their function to put the whole apostolic message in the light of the Old Testament? Or did they concentrate on transmitting the words of the Lord in their teaching? One can also think of the whole apostolic and communal tradition that was soon crystallized in definite narratives and formulae. Perhaps they drew occasionally on their own revelation, charismatically received, and transmitted new insights into the truth. Or were they more concerned with the moral demands put to people on the basis of the Gospel and the ecclesial community? There is no doubt that they also played a role in the liturgical gatherings of the People of God (Acts 13, 1).

Do we have to choose between all these possibilities? Could they not have coexisted, all of them? Could they not all be interconnected? Could they not easily slide one into the other?

Two points are clear in any case. The first is that the teachers, too, were there to build up the community, the whole. The second is that from the beginning Christianity emphasized the truth and the knowledge of the truth.

This latter point is fundamental. The community lived by a message, the apostolic kerygma. This message related to historical events, and therefore to the reality of the created world. It was in these events that the whole Old Testament found its fulfillment, not only the words of the Old Testament but also the reality of Israel's history. Jesus was an historical figure; his words and deeds, his way and his work, had a decisive importance for salvation. The Spirit was not a creature of phantasy but related to this reality in all his activity. Nor was he chaotic; he taught how to speak of this reality of salvation in definite and clear judgments and statements; the truth of this reality had to be proclaimed. On this depended the whole sanity of the spiritual life. It was pervaded by a strong discipline of soundness, intelligibility, simplicity, sobriety and clear-headedness. This stating of the truth could happen in various ways, as a proclamation or a narrative or an explanation or as applied, or by way of instruction or apologetics. In all these ways it would guide and build up.

Tradition added many things and dropped others. In the old Church, the later Middle Ages and the Churches of the Reformation the teacher returned as preacher, the servant of the Word. The heart of the matter then becomes not so much the fact that "the Church" formulates, proclaims and proposes things to believe. Preaching is not purely concerned with truth as such, but with the truth as saving, as the message of deliverance for sinners. One can even recognize a considerable distance between the apostolic kerygma as the historical and prophetic message about actual salvation and the ecclesiastical dogma as the projection of this message and its content into rational thought. And if one then sees, as the Reformation did, the only way of making salvation present to be the apostolic function of preaching, and not the sacraments, the teacher acquires on the one hand, a wholly specific (purely kerygmatic) and on the other, a decisive character (since his function is the only form of transmitting salvation).

However, the preacher is not only teacher but also prophet and *episkopos* or presbyter—in a word, practically the whole "apostle" continues to live in the preacher. On the other hand, the teacher is not only continued by the preacher. Apart from preaching there was, since early days, the catechesis. This has always had a double aspect. It transmits the truth of salvation as an historical reality, first of all, to posterity, the children born of believing parents who, as their "offspring", belong to the Church by virtue of the covenant, and second, to outsiders who, for reasons unknown to us, are interested in the teaching and community of the Church and in the Gospel of Christ, which makes them wish to belong, too. In the course of centuries, the catechist has been embodied in a multitude of ways, but he continues as "teacher" in a way peculiarly his own.

II

VARIOUS FUNCTIONS

A totally different set of factors, however, made him undergo a modification that was only present in the New Testament in a very modest and embryonic fashion. I see four of these factors. There is, first of all, the possibility of heresy within the Church. This heresy is an experiment in thought that failed. A man, school or movement tries to think anew the truth of the Gospel (Who is Jesus? What is salvation? etc.) and to state this afresh. There is every reason for such experiments: Did the Church ever succeed in expressing this truth completely and totally in a pure and intelligible manner? But the experimenter loses his way in the jungle. He drops essential things, exaggerates others. The teacher becomes a teacher of error. And this, in any case, breaks off the succession, the continuity of the teachers. Other teachers appear in order to combat the heresy. This combat is in itself already a powerful stimulus for the teacher to make progress in his own development. Gradually the theologian is born.

The second factor is that this development leads the teacher to become also an apologist. He justifies the hope that lives in him. He does this before outsiders who attack the content of his faith and ridicule it. Over against this he tries to show that to believe in the Christian sense is not quite so ridiculous. He examines its credibility. He even uses the weapons of his opponents, namely, the laws of reason and the facts of reality. He may also proceed to an attack and fight the opinions of his opponents, also with their own weapons. In brief, as an apologist, the teacher adds reason and the secular reality to revelation and faith, while growing as a theologian.

The third factor is of a higher kind. It concerns the confrontation of a thinking Christendom (concentrated in the teachers) with other religions, with philosophy and the whole of culture, in science and art, law and reason. Is there only untruth in those fields? Are such fields completely dominated by demons? Or are there also elements that could be accepted and integrated, or at least "baptized" and christianized? Should the Christian not enter into that culture, though without surrendering himself to it? Is a synthesis impossible? Is it not part of the Church's catholicity to bring about such a synthesis? This issue becomes urgent when we look at the State. At the beginning one had to witness before Pontius Pilate, at the risk of one's life. This presupposed that one had some idea of the truth, the true doctrine, the right formula, and this required a teacher. Later Pontius Pilate himself came to witness. This put the Church in a totally new position and gave her a new responsibility in or toward the State. As guardian of the Gospel and the law, the Church became the source where the water of truth bubbled up for the State! Without that synthesis of Gospel and culture the Church could not possibly fulfill that function.

The fourth factor is the most important. Even as a believing Christian man remains a creature who has to think, he has to penetrate into the mysteries of salvation as a reality. He wants to be as clear as possible about these mysteries. Moreover, he wants to connect these mysteries with the mysteries of man's specifically human existence and the whole existence of created reality. Did Paul and John already dream of this? Or were they simply full of the ineffable gift of salvation? What is here the place of those lesser gods of the New Testament, the teachers? We do not know. The Bible does not tell us much about it. But Origen had already begun to tackle this in the grand style. Since then the vision of an all-embracing rational synthesis has always enthralled the Church. The importance of this for missionary preaching and all preaching directed to those outside the pale can hardly be exaggerated.

III

THE TEACHER, THE REFORMER AND THE MAN OF SCIENCE

The Reformation was an incident in the tradition of the universal Church that again added a totally new emphasis to this perspective. It brought out the function of the servant of the Word and of preaching as the outstanding means of transmitting salvation. But this is not my point here. The Reformation was brought about by the *reformer*. Luther and Calvin saw themselves and each other as having a wholly extraordinary function, inspired by God, namely, that of a reformer who is as close to the apostle as the teacher of 1 Corinthians 12, 28. For Calvin Luther is an "apostolic man". He sees himself as a "doctor of Holy Scripture". He even dares speak of "my dogma" (that of justification of the godless by faith alone).

Thus the *teacher* suddenly became the *reformer,* the reformer of the Church and of the Christian religion at that, and this on the basis of Holy Scripture, if necessary even against the authority of the legal and functional establishment. But it is seen in such a way that the prophetic ferment of Holy Scripture does not interrupt the tradition, but rather continues it, as it were, by an acceleration in the current of tradition. As teacher of Holy Scripture, the teacher then becomes the teacher of the Church in a most exceptional manner: within Scripture he stands so to speak above the Church and shows her the way, back to the sources and forward to a new phase in history.

But this is an exception and incidental. The Reformation never intended that the Church should be teeming with reformers. The servant of the Word as "pastor and teacher" moves already at a much lower level as "teacher" in the Church. This does not prevent that possibility of the "teacher-reformer" from complicating enormously the question of the succession of the teachers. This complication makes it in any case impossible to treat this succession as a matter of purely logical continuity. Insofar as the teacher is concerned, this cannot be found anywhere. We have but to recall the modifications undergone by the teacher when he began to combat heresy, concentrated on apologetics, attempted to bring about a cultural synthesis and tried to embrace all in a system of rational thought.

A new complication appeared in modern times. There has always been a need for the training and schooling of the servants of the Church. The history of this process is beyond the scope of this article. The one feature I want to stress is that this training naturally ended up in a "school", in the framework of *science,* somewhat restricted in the seminary, with more freedom in the Catholic university, and left totally (or almost totally) to itself in the State university. There are some today who would like to abandon the "apartheid" character of the whole of theology, the theology faculty included, and would like it to adopt, like the Church herself, the incognito style of the world in the way the other sciences and faculties do this. Then the "teacher" has completely disappeared; he is then no longer necessary. In this context they then usually see Christianity simply as an implicit and anonymous way of existence.

For the time being, however, we are not likely to lose the professor of theology. And with him the theologian as such will keep his position. There is even a strong tendency to give the theologian as such a social function, in other words, not to dress him up as an official of the Church.

In the meantime, the scientific theologian as a variant of the teacher, has enough problems as it is. Is theology still possible as a genuine free science? Is there not an abyss between the historico-critical method of science and systematic, dogmatic theology? Is the treatment of everything as a rational problem not typical of science and how do we reconcile this with the certainty of faith, which was the very root of the original teacher? Can the Church ever renounce every ecclesiastical and confessional control of a theological faculty? Is this kind of control not merely an explicitation of what is always present implicitly and is it not a condition for a treatment of the matter in a way worthy of man?

Whether the theologian as such, and the professor of theology in particular, has a special function in the Church is a matter that has been given much thought in the course of centuries, without much result. Here we should remember the question whether there is a single function in the Church which is purely a function. Are not all functions together, originating from the apostolic function, primarily functions in the kingdom of God? Has even authority not been seen in the perspective of apostolic succession, as has happened since Constantine? Is it then not enough for the professor of theology to have a functional position in the cultural framework?

This would also diminish the sharp distinction from the laity. In a certain sense all the faithful are theologians. The science of theology, in that sense, is the most democratic and popular of all sciences. What is the *agens,* the operative factor, in the development of teaching within the Church's tradition—Holy Scripture? The Word incarnate? The Christian sense (*ratio christiana*) of the People of God, enlightened by the Spirit? As theologian, the teacher stands, in any case, right in the middle of the community, while, as preacher, his position is in contrast with this community.

This leads us to another problem. How great is the distance between the Gospel as the message of salvation for the lost children of man as it is preached to them, and the dogma or confession, which is a confessing response to this message or a penetration of this message with the light of reason? And how great is the distance between dogma or confession on the one hand and the myriad theological statements on the other which are mainly an indulging in the refined cultural game of rationalizing, somewhat lightly playing with every possible kind of question, though also sincerely trying to labor at new formulations of dogma and trying to build up a philosophy of the revelation with a serious apologetic or synthesizing effort?

The teacher who has completely become a theologian finds his material mainly in these *theologoumena,* these theological statements, particularly today when all kinds of new things are being thought about, such as a God who is dead.

With all this, the question remains: Is there a succession, a continuity, of teachers? I believe that every systematic theologian realizes that the tradition of theological thought throughout the centuries is the only water in which he can swim. A systematic theology, divorced from the history of theology (and dogma), is, in spite of its frequently fascinating acrobatics, merely a fish out of water. Every good teacher in Christianity is aware of the deep spiritual bonds that bind him to all his predecessors. But what is the nature, the structure of this continuity? Are there no "leaps"? Are there no contrasts and contradictions? Can one just lump together all that the teachers have thought and said so far? Do we not have to choose? If we understand tradition and continuity as the gift and work of the Spirit, it is much easier to allow for "leaps" and contradictions than when we see it purely as an unfolding of the Word incarnate. The continuity remains but allows for enormous elasticity. The Spirit moves even through contradictions; it pursues and leads into the whole truth, which is eschatological by nature. That is why every teacher needs all his predecessors and can make use of all of them. If we base ourselves on the incarnate Word, we could not put all this in the same way since, by nature, it proceeds very differently, also with regard to continuity.

Is this succession of teachers also an apostolic succession? At the beginning of this article we already saw that the teacher stands closer to the apostle than the *episkopoi* and the presbyters. I also mentioned how the apostle belongs to the kingdom before he belongs to the Church. How can we, in view of these two facts, avoid speaking of an apostolic succession in the full sense, not only along the lines of bishops or of official gatherings, but also *via* the teachers? We should of course remember that many modifications have taken place between the apostle and the professor of theology. But there can be no doubt that something of the apostolic authority accrues to the theological scholar. He, too, seeks and finds the truth that is in Christ.

The great question that remains concerns who has the final word? Who determines the teaching of the Church? Who exercises the doctrinal discipline? Must new dogmas be declared? What is the validity of the dogmas of tradition? One thing seems to me to be absolutely certain: In the Christian faith we cannot do without doctrine, confession and dogma. It is too strongly based on a reality that is historical and on a truth that must be proclaimed. Even when we see Christianity and Church merely as a way of being and acting in the world, we still must have the true, the genuine way of being and acting (*orthopraxis*). We need at least an ethical teaching. But the Christian cannot limit himself to that. Such a concept is too exclusively "civil". The soteriological and ontological issues remain too sharply alive in Christianity. In this it also guarantees the noblest values of man and culture: it is not merely a matter of goodness and beauty, but also of truth and salvation.

But who decides these questions in the end? The teachers in their apostolic succession? The teacher has grown into a theologian. In theology, especially when taken as a science, there lurks an enormous danger for the Church. It can tyrannize the Church, even unto death. That is why it is on the whole not such a happy situation if all the Church's officials are qualified theologians or even people merely scientifically trained in theology. In that situation the teacher then ousts, and in many ways, all the other apostolic functions in the Church. The presbyteral and synodal system of Church government therefore fortunately maintains, side by side with theologically trained servants of the Word, elders and deacons who are laymen from the theological point of view but fully fledged functionaries from the ecclesial point of view. In this system the decision-making is done by the official gatherings where the three functions meet to decide upon the government of the Church (through Christ).

We should also remember that teaching, in the Christian and ecclesial sense, not only ethical teaching but also soteriological and ontological doctrine, lies essentially embedded in the reality of the lived Christian life and historical salvation. The mystical and the liturgical elements, the sacramental and the social, the prophetic (preaching) and the communal (*koinonia*), the mystical union with Christ and the indwelling of the Holy Spirit, the life of faith and of love—all these elements together constitute the essence of the Church. Seen in this light, teaching is no more than an intellectual ripple on this vast sea of reality. In the development and maintenance of doctrine the teachers, particularly as theologians, can only give their labor and serve. The decision must lie with those who *ex officio* are informed about the fullness of the Church's reality.

Bernard Dupuy, O.P. / *Etiolles, France*

Is There a Dogmatic Distinction between the Function of Priests and the Function of Bishops?

Must we say, on the basis of Trent, Vatican I and Vatican II, that there is a dogmatic difference between the priesthood and the episcopate? Some theologians, impressed by the testimony of tradition from the 2nd century onward and by more recent reaffirmation of the sacramentality of the episcopate, are inclined to say that there is such a difference. However, none of the conciliar declarations invoked in this matter have a dogmatic character; so we must take a closer look at them.

I

THE CONCILIAR DOCUMENTS

What is the import of Trent's decree? In canons 6 and 7 of the *Decree on the Sacrament of Orders* (*De sacramento ordinis*, session XXIII, July 15, 1563), it recalls the fact that there are "orders" which structure the ecclesiastical ministry:

> *Canon 6:* "If anyone says that there is not a divinely instituted hierarchy in the Catholic Church, comprising bishops, priests and ministers, let him be anathema . . ."
>
> *Canon 7:* "If anyone says that bishops are not superior to priests: or that they do not have the power to confirm and

74

ordain: or that they have it in common with priests: or that the orders which they confer are illicit without the consent or the appeal of the people and the secular power: or that those who are not ordained and sent legitimately by the ecclesiastical, canonical authorities are legitimate ministers of the Word and the sacraments, let him be anathema." [1]

Clearly the Council of Trent affirmed the superiority of bishops to priests insofar as the *power of orders* is concerned. The above texts are the most decisive to be invoked in favor of a dogmatic distinction. But right here we must ask whether Trent set out to settle the precise question we are asking today. Did it intend to talk about a dogmatic distinction based on revelation and clearly fixed for the entire lifetime of the Church? Did it aim to settle dogmatically the classification of ministerial tasks such as we know it today?

A. Duval has clearly shown[2] that the fathers of Trent never had this intention. It seems that their only intention was to affirm that there are orders (*ordines*) within the ecclesiastical ministry. Chapter IV is perfectly clear on this point: the ecclesiastical ministry is not based on the universal priesthood of the faithful and does not derive from it; all Christians do not share the same spiritual power equally and indiscriminately (*promiscue*); in the Church there are diverse charisms and functions, in accordance with an arrangement that derives from the apostles. Moreover, bishops exercise certain sacramental functions that priests cannot carry out. That is the precise teaching of Trent. Thus Trent's decree is related to the larger question we are asking here, but it is an answer to questions which the Council fathers had to tackle in their own day. To answer our question, they would have had to define episcopacy and priesthood; this they did not do.

Vatican I had made provisions to broach the question in its schema on the Church (*De Ecclesia*). Kleutgen, who drew up a draft of the text, planned to go a little further than Trent; he planned to say that bishops are superior to priests in order and

[1] *DS.* 1776–77.
[2] A. Duval, "L'Ordre au Concile de Trente," in *Etudes sur le Sacrement de l'Ordre* (Paris: Editions du Cerf, 1957), pp. 305–8.

jurisdiction (*tam ordine quam jurisdictione*).³ If this text had been adopted, the new element introduced would have been this: Vatican I would have affirmed that the bishop's superiority over the priest is by *divine right (de jure divino)*.⁴

Kleutgen went all out to affirm the superiority of episcopal jurisdiction over that of priests. Yet it is worth noting that he states that he has no intention of determining the nature of episcopal jurisdiction; he also leaves open the question of the origin of this jurisdiction, which was debated at Trent. Clearly, then, Kleutgen's draft does not provide a dogmatic response to our question—the distinction between the priesthood and the episcopate.

There is no doubt that Vatican II adopted a new outlook on the question we have posed. In discussing the formation of the Church in general, and the priesthood in particular, Vatican II refers back to the New Testament and ancient tradition rather than to more recent conciliar texts.⁵ One need only recall its essential stance on several matters: the Church as the People of God, the priesthood of the faithful, the charismatic aspect of the Church, the Church as a communion of local Churches, the ministry as service. Trent spoke essentially of the *hierarchy,* and it linked the *establishment* of the threefold ministry (bishops, priests, deacons) to divine *ordination*. Vatican II does not deny this (it cites Trent), but it is more circumspect in its wording: "The *ecclesiastical ministry, established* by God, is *exercised* on different levels by those who, from ancient times, have been called bishops, priests and deacons." ⁶

In short, Trent makes a simple theological affirmation that is based on tradition; Vatican II chooses to be more attentive to the data of history and to present-day ecumenical realities. The statements of Trent are meant to be a reminder; those of Vatican II try to be attentive to the context, as is indicated by several notes of the theological commission which were appended to

---

³ Vatican I, *De Ecclesia,* Chapter IV: De ecclesiastica hierarchia.
⁴ Cf. Mansi 53, 321 A–B.
⁵ Cf. the notes in the *Constitution on the Church,* chap. IV.
⁶ *Constitution on the Church,* n. 28.

the text. We shall get back to these notes later. Right now we need only remember that while the texts of Vatican II do not have the imperative form of Trent's canons, they do have greater dogmatic import. Why? Because they regard the ecclesial institution in continuity from its very beginnings and in terms of its present situation in the world.

II

MEDIEVAL THEOLOGY

Investigations into the history of doctrine and canon law have revealed the impact of medieval thought on our theology of the priesthood. Pre-Scholastic theologians and canonists inherited two currents of thought. They tried to harmonize these two currents, but Gratian was not able to integrate them fully.

The first was a doctrinal current that went back to St. Jerome,[7] Ambrosiaster and Pelagius. It entered the medieval fabric through Isidore of Seville and Gratian. This doctrinal current stressed the equality of bishops and priests within one single priesthood. It affirms that the distinction between priests and bishops is of late invention and based solely on ecclesiastical law. If certain powers are "reserved" to the bishop, this simply means that they are "bound" in the priest.

A second current of thought, represented by the canonists, is to be found in Pseudo-Isidore and the Decretals. It affirms that the distinction between priests of the first and second rank is of divine origin,[8] dating back to the distinction between the selection of twelve apostles and that of seventy-two disciples.

In the 11th and 12th centuries, theologians and canonists tried to bridge the contradiction between these two viewpoints. This they did with the help of the Dionysian theory of the hierarchy

[7] Cf. *Ep. ad Titum* I, 5; *P.L.* 26, 579ff., passed into law in c. 5, D 35, ed. Friedberg I, 332ff; *Ep. 146 ad Evangelium, P.L.* 22, 1191–95, passed into law in c. 24, D 99, ed. Friedberg I, 327ff.

[8] Cf. *Collectio Decretalium,* Ep. 66 Leonis Papae, *P.L.* 130, 881.

and their own canonical conceptions. This gave rise, in the 11th century, to the distinction between *ordo* and *officium* (or *potestas*) and, a little later, to the distinction between *ordo* and *jurisdictio*.[9]

Now during this whole period the only question being asked concerned the *sacerdotal ministry*. People started from the principle that only one ministry had been instituted and that it was diversified in its actual exercise. Since the eucharist was the supreme moment for the fulfillment of this ministry, their whole theology of orders was constructed in terms of the eucharistic celebration. But it became difficult to pinpoint an exact place for the episcopate and the diaconate; gradually people forgot that the first was a sacrament, and the specific character of the second became blurred.

In our day we have come to realize that we must recapture the full plenitude of orders, and this has renewed our interest in the diaconate and the episcopate. But we must be wary of one thing: if we do not start from Scripture and the life of the Church, if we do not take into account the reality of *ministries* in the Church, then we may falsely regard the episcopate and the diaconate as splinterings of the one priestly ministry.

The modern word "ministry" has a broader sense than the classical word "ministerium"; the latter meant "sacerdotal ministry". To resolve our present problem, then, it seems we shall have to move beyond the distinction between order and jurisdiction. Some do say that the distinction between bishop and priest is solely one of jurisdiction; others would like to base the difference on divine institution, so that there would be a difference in orders as well. But it seems to me that neither of these two viewpoints takes adequate account of the reality under investigation. They do not take adequate account of history, particularly of the history of the Church and her origins; and this history has suddenly become something close to us with our renewed ecumenical awareness. So here, too, we must return to the sources.

[9] Cf. P. de Alcantara, "Función episcopal en la Iglesia primitiva," in *Teología del Episcopado*, Spanish Theology Week, 22 (Madrid, 1963), pp. 217–53; cf. *Rev. Sc. Ph. et Th.*, 49 (1965), pp. 305–08, 320–22.

III

THE DOCTRINE OF THE MINISTRY IN THE NEW TESTAMENT

The biblical revival and the current ecumenical context have made clear to us that any study of the Church's ministry must start with the ministry of Christ himself. We must study his ministry, and then examine the relationship between the Church's ministries and his ministry.[10]

Jesus Christ declared that he would be *actively present* among his followers both during his earthly ministry and afterward. During his earthly ministry he told them: "He who receives you, receives me; and he who receives me, receives him who sent me" (Mt. 10, 40); "He who hears you, hears me" (Lk. 10, 16). These sentiments are echoed in his farewell promise: "I am with you all days, even unto the consummation of the world" (Mt. 28, 20). In this sense, Christ's disciples today are living testimony to his presence; they are his deputies and representatives. As Karl Barth put it: "To deny in principle the concept *Vicarius Christi* would lead to a denial of the notion *Christus praesens*." [11]

There is an active, sacramental presence of Christ in his Church, and it is expressed in the community of life between him and his apostles. This community of life was begun during his earthly life; it was cemented during his passover, with the last supper and their confession of faith. It is manifested through the gift of the Holy Spirit, through charisms and through the fact that the disciples have been vested with a certain power (according to the New Testament): "Whatever you bind on earth shall be bound also in heaven" (Mt. 18, 18). Even before we interpret this formula (and others like it) as the conferral of some particular power of "jurisdiction", we must read it as a general affirmation of stewardship and vigilance over the community. In short, it speaks of a *ministry* exercised *in the name of Christ*. The ministry exercised in Christ's name is a manifestation of his presence

[10] Cf., for example, K. H. Schelkle, *Disciple et apôtre* (Tübingen, 1961, Paris: ed. Mappus, 1965).

[11] K. Barth, *Kirchliche Dogmatik*, I/I, p. 93 (Eng. tr.: *Church Dogmatics*, 4 vols.) (New York, 1936–1962).

in his Church. That is the basic teaching of the New Testament on the ministry.

The pastoral epistles go further. Mirroring a later era in the life of the Christian community, they speak of a *succession* in this ministry which is exercised in the name of Christ. The word "succession" (*diadochē, successio*) is not in the New Testament, but we do find the idea that doctrine is transmitted and preserved faithfully by virtue of a continuity of witnesses (2 Tim. 2, 2). This is one of the characteristic points in the pastoral epistles according to Protestant exegetes, who regard it as a twist in the primitive doctrine and the first trace of a "Pre-Catholicism".

According to the pastoral epistles, faithful transmission of the faith is insured by a "line of succession" that operates among the witnesses sent to preach the Gospel. Nothing in the pastoral epistles, however, allows us to say that it is through consecration or ordination that these witnesses undertake to fulfill their ministry as the apostles fulfilled it. One might well assume this, but the point is that neither Christ nor his apostles expressly and definitively fixed the forms, the structure, and the limits of this ministry. The New Testament does not provide us with a ministerial setup that has precise institutional form.

In ecumenical discussions today we find more and more agreement on this point: the ecclesiastical ministry is not completely determined by the statements of the New Testament. The New Testament bears witness to *various* ministries. But we cannot speak of *the* ministry without appealing to Tradition as well. Even for Protestant theologians, the question of the ministry is not a purely scriptural one; while all Christian denominations appeal to Scripture on this point, their conceptions of the ministry are also colored by historical factors and their confessional preconceptions. While they may justifiably claim to have the "essential" ministry, they cannot claim that only their exercise of this ministry is in perfect "conformity to Scripture" because the ministerial setup cannot be fixed decisively on the basis of Scripture alone.[12]

[12] Cf. Schlink, in *Kerygma und Dogma*, 1961, pp. 105–07. H. d'Espine, text cited in *Istina*, 8 (1961–62), p. 360, note 5.

Thus we must get beyond the principle of *sola scriptura,* if there is to be ecumenical progress on the question of the ministry. We can only move forward if everyone recognizes that the ecclesiastical ministry depends on both Scripture and Tradition. Progress on this question requires progress on the hermeneutical question.

As far as the scriptural side of the question is concerned, we cannot determine the ministerial setup on the basis of the pastoral epistles alone; it must be investigated, not only in terms of the complete canon of Scripture, but also in terms of the central reality in Scripture: the ministry of Christ, which is the touchstone and the model for any ecclesiastical ministry. And hermeneutically speaking, this central reality brings up the question of Tradition. An understanding of the ministry comes through the Church; its setup results from a determination that is both apostolic and post-apostolic.

From a dogmatic viewpoint, the status of the ministry can be compared to the canon of Scripture. Several people have pointed this out.[13] Hence it is no longer a question of establishing the relationship between bishop and priest on the express words of Christ. The real question is whether, in the light of the way the ministerial functions have been fixed over the course of time, bishops and priests really do exercise the essential functions which Christ conferred on his apostles.

IV

DOGMATIC VALUE OF THE THREEFOLD SETUP
(BISHOP, PRIEST, DEACON)

Like the canon of Scripture and the limitation of the sacraments to seven, the threefold division of the ecclesiastical ministry (episcopate, priesthood, diaconate) can be viewed as a matter of Church *development.* This basic arrangement could be formulated theologically and actually practiced only as the Church

[13] Cf. R. Paquier, text cited in *Istina,* 9 (1963), p. 178; A. M. Ramsey, *The Gospel and the Catholic Church* (London, 1936), p. 63.

moved from apostolic times into the 2nd century. Nevertheless, according to the Catholic view on its institution, it continues to have a *de jure* character. There will always be deacons, a ministry of elders, a ministry of supervision. With regard to the concrete forms taken by this essential structure, they obviously can vary greatly with the times, and they have in fact. Indeed, they should vary by virtue of their historical nature and by virtue of their obligation to remain in conformity with the ministry Christ assigned to his apostles.

Let me emphasize the point once again. The New Testament does not provide us with a normative structure for the ministry, one fixed definitively for the lifetime of the Church, one which all present-day Christian communions should adopt forthwith. The only ministry we know, the one that has been handed down to us by Tradition, is one which has been subject to development.

The Catholic Church is the historical Church willed by Jesus Christ, but not in the sense that her present-day ministry is the one and only historical form of the ministry willed by him. The ministry of the Catholic Church indeed bears witness to an essential datum—the episcopate-priesthood-diaconate theology (retained by Trent and Vatican II [14]—but its present-day form is not to be identified necessarily, in theology or practice, with that essential datum.

The form of bishop-priest relationship we know today was preceded by other types of this same relationship. Today it is thought that "bishop" related to Greek communities and "priest" to Jewish communities; but the pastoral epistles themselves already seem to bear witness to a bishop-priest ministry on the way toward unification.[15] The monarchical episcopate soon asserted itself almost everywhere. At the end of the 2nd century, in St. Irenaeus and the *Traditio apostolica,* we find that the monarchical bishop is regarded as the inheritor of the apostles' functions and as the

[14] *DS.* 1776; *Constitution on the Church,* n. 28.
[15] Cf. P. Benoît, "Les origines de l'Episcopat selon le Nouveau Testament," in *L'Eglise du Christ* (Paris, 1963), pp. 13–57. Text cited in the *Relatio* on the schema *De Ecclesia,* nn. 28, 101.

guardian of Tradition; we still have priests, but they do not have this function of being the apostles' successors.

In the Africa of Tertullian and Cyprian, only the bishop is called *sacerdos* and celebrates the eucharist; priests, who now seem to have only a pastoral function of governing, no longer preside over the eucharist. After the Council of Nicaea in the 4th century, however, this situation reverses itself once again. Priests are *sacerdotes* once again and celebrate the eucharist for the bishop in his territory. The bishop becomes the head of a *presbyterium* and the pastor of an entire region; we already have the territorial bishop which we know today.

The conclusion is that the process of differentiating between bishop and priest has been a varied and progressive one. Fixed at Antioch at the end of the 1st century, the specific nature of the episcopal ministry was definitively recognized only in the 2nd century when Gnosticism posed a challenge; it was recognized everywhere later, as the result of the crisis caused by the priest Arius.

With this changing history in the background, it is easy to see why Vatican II, desiring to respect this history and the present ecumenical situation, chose to avoid dogmatic definition of a particular structure. In the *Constitution on the Church,* it calls the episcopate "the apex of the sacred ministry" (n. 21), but it chose not to declare dogmatically that only bishops can call priests to become members of the episcopal college. The older formula of this principle was: "Quare soli Episcopi per Sacramentum Ordinis novos electos in corpus episcopale assumere *possunt*; Vatican II substitutes for this a simple statement of fact: "Episcoporum *est* per Sacramentum Ordinis novos electos in corpus episcopale assumere."

Vatican II thus left open the possibility of personal judgment on the historical facts. (In the Church of Alexandria, for example, the college of priests seems to have chosen its own bishop for several decades.) It obviously wanted to avoid creating ecumenical difficulties at a time when various Churches were talking about reunion. It also wanted to leave room for the case, however hypothetical it may be, where priests are isolated for a long time without a bishop because of Church persecution. Most importantly, it wanted to avoid making a dogmatic determination on a point of doctrine that is far from settled.

For these various reasons, based on Scripture and/or historical fact, we are led to avoid affirming a rigorously dogmatic difference between the episcopate and the priesthood. What consequences does this decision have in terms of the theology of the sacrament of orders?

V

THEOLOGICAL ASPECT

Trent based its theological treatment of holy orders on the Epistle to the Hebrews. It teaches that the apostles were made *priests* by our Lord at the last supper, when he instituted the eucharistic sacrifice. Thus holy orders is a *sacrament instituted* by Christ (session XXIII, chap. I). Moreover, there are several established orders, *each* by ordination (chap. II).

Present-day theologians know that it is very difficult to furnish scriptural proof for this tridentine theology. The most direct theological *locus* for the ministry in the New Testament is not the Epistle to the Hebrews. Moreover, one cannot say with certainty that Paul's imposition of hands on Timothy—regularly invoked in favor of the ordination of ministers—was an episcopal consecration distinct from his ordinations to the priesthood (1 Tim. 4, 14; 5, 22; 2 Tim. 1, 6). Today we are more inclined to think that at the beginning there were *two* rites of installation.[16]

Instead of basing the hierarchy of orders on actual institution as Trent does, it seems more in keeping with Scripture to start with the Church, the "original sacrament", as K. Rahner, O. Semmelroth, E. H. Schillebeeckx and others now do. In this way holy orders is not isolated from the historical Church and somehow placed above it; orders is a dimension of the Church.

[16] Cf. *Rev. Sc. Ph. et Th.*, 49 (1965), pp. 289–90.

The Church is the embodiment, the visible manifestation, of Christ's active yet mysterious presence. The Church is the primordial sacrament, and each "sacrament" is one aspect of this manifestation. A sacrament is a fundamental action of the Church, essential to her existence, even though we have only now begun to reflect on the specific character of each sacrament in terms of its relationship to the nature of the Church herself. A given sacrament could have been instituted directly by Christ. But it is also possible, and it is true in the case of several sacraments, that they do not derive from some explicit word of institution spoken by Christ. Holy orders and marriage are two instances. "Jesus instituted the ministry in the Church. But he did not leave us any explicit word of his own on its sacramental character." [17]

Orders, nevertheless, is part of the essence of the Church. It is an action through which the Church realizes her being; it is in this sense that orders is, properly speaking, a sacrament.

If this is the case, we can set down certain guidelines:

(a) The validity of the sacraments is tied up with the activity of the Church, not with a sacramental act taken in isolation.[18]

(b) The diversification of orders into several ranks and the establishment of diverse ordinations has been effected by the Church herself, at the very least, in the case of the separation of episcopate and priesthood.[19] Thus whether we should speak of one sacrament of orders or of two is a terminological question. It is a theological differentiation, not a dogmatic distinction.[20]

(c) Finally, it seems impossible to establish theologically a radical difference between the functions of the bishop and those of the priest. To repeat, it is a difference established in law, but it is not absolute and immutable.

We find proof for this in the power to confirm and ordain. Trent reserved the power to confirm to bishops. Yet

[17] K. Rahner, *Kirch und Sakramente* (Herder, 1960), p. 44 (*Eng. tr.: Church and the Sacraments,* New York: Herder and Herder, 1963).
[18] *Ibid.,* p. 59.
[19] *Ibid.,* p. 51.
[20] *Ibid.*

ancient Tradition, Eastern Tradition to the present day, and
the decisions of Rome in 1946 accord this power to priests.
As for ordination, historians have found several cases where
simple priests were called upon to perform ordinations ha-
bitually reserved to bishops.[21]

The only way to square these facts and these variations
in Church discipline is to regard the functions of the priest
as a toning down of the bishop's functions. Their power, of
itself, is radically identical (*potestas ordinis*), but ordinarily
it is *bound* (*potestas legata*).

At the present time we cannot go beyond these assertions.
In the last analysis, is the difference between the episcopate and
the priesthood one of divine law or one of ecclesiastical law?
Formulated this way, the distinction seems too absolute and
entirely inadequate. It runs along two levels of law, and it does
not belong exclusively to one or the other. Vatican II took cog-
nizance of the complex status of orders in the Church. Its position
suggests that we should not consider the distinction between
bishops and priests as being purely one of divine law, and that
we should pay close attention to the ministry's roots in history
and in the Church. The ministerial setup in the Church—apostolic succession and the episcopal ministry in particular—are not
firmly fixed in the New Testament; it is a setup founded in the
New Testament, carried on by Tradition, and established to
perdure as the ministry of *the Church* and the ministry *willed by
Jesus Christ* for his disciples.

[21] Cf. Y. Congar, "Faits, problèmes et réflexions à propos du pouvoir
d'ordre et des rapports entre le presbytérat et l'episcopat," in *La Maison-
Dieu*, 14, pp. 107–28. Reprinted in *Sainte-Eglise* (Paris, 1965), pp.
275–302.

Maurice Villain, S.M./*Paris, France*

Can There Be Apostolic Succession outside the Chain of Imposition of Hands?

This question was simply not asked before the advent of the era of ecumenism. In our classical teaching[1] one thought of the apostolic succession as a kind of genealogical descent that linked a bishop or priest to the twelve apostles and Christ by means of an uninterrupted chain of impositions of hands. Once this sacramental gesture was duly performed by a member of the hierarchy, the candidate received from Christ himself the ministerial priesthood, in its fullness with the power to ordain in his turn, if it was an episcopal consecration; as a subordinate share, if it was a simple ordination to the priesthood.

The consequences of this wholly juridical position are serious. The laity, who do not receive this imposition of hands, can in no way be enabled to exercise the pastoral ministry. As to the Protestant pastor, who receives it from one or more already ordained ministers but outside the line of hierarchical descent, he is considered to be cut off from this succession and the acts of his ministry are, apart from baptism, held to be invalid. In any case, he is not interested in the way we judge him since he does not recognize this descent from the apostles, and the ministerial

[1] I am not saying "in the Church's Tradition" for reasons that will be obvious later on.

priesthood is, to him, superfluous: baptism alone confers on the "People of God" that "royal (or ecclesial) priesthood", and there is no other.

These two positions are radically opposed. It is therefore hardly astonishing that our usual catechetics bypasses the profound meaning and real content of the imposition of hands and only looks at the somewhat magical result. As long as the rite is accomplished by a validly consecrated bishop and with the "intention to do what the Church does", the candidate is validly ordained; if not, then there is no ordination. In case of doubt—and who can be sure that there has never been a break in this chain either on the part of the act or on that of the intention?—we have recourse to our *Ecclesia supplet* (the Church supplies what is missing). Such a simplification had two results: it established a separation of the clerical world from that of the laity, with an unfortunate subordination of the second to the first, and it created a disastrous difference of level between the Catholic priest and the Protestant pastor so that what a pastor could be in his ontological reality was of no interest to the priest who treated him rather as a poor relation, and hence if a dialogue were at all possible on the basis of friendship, the position was already distorted at the root.

Hence, the importance of the question: To what degree and in what sense can we speak of an apostolic succession outside the chain of imposition of hands? It is revealing that Vatican II itself prompts us to ask that question. It is indeed implied (at least indirectly) in many conciliar texts, supported by references to Scripture. The scope of this article does not allow me to quote all those texts and I shall limit myself to their general trend and the positive conclusion it leads to. We shall then see that this conclusion makes us touch the most tender points in our dialogue with the Protestant Churches and ask ourselves questions that have hardly been examined. In the second half I shall therefore try to answer those questions or at least show the direction in which we must look for an answer.

I

THE POSITIVE INDICATIONS TO BE FOUND IN VATICAN II

The texts of Vatican II fall into two groups. One group concerns the royal priesthood of those who are baptized (*Constitution on the Church* and *Decree on the Apostolate of the Laity.* The other group concerns the Churches and ecclesial communities which sprang from the Reformation (*Decree on Ecumenism*).

1. *Texts Dealing with the Royal Priesthood of the Baptized*

One ought to read the whole of chapter II on "The People of God" in the *Constitution on the Church*. I limit myself to n. 10, which clearly shows the biblical foundation of this teaching:[2]

> Christ the Lord, high priest taken from among men (cf. Heb. 5, 1–5), "made a kingdom and priests to God his Father" (Apoc. 1, 6; cf. 5, 9–10) out of this new people. The baptized, by regeneration and the anointing of the Holy Spirit, are consecrated into a spiritual house and a holy priesthood. Thus through all those works befitting Christian men they can offer spiritual sacrifices and proclaim the power of him who has called them out of darkness into his marvelous light (cf. 1 Pet. 2, 4–10). Therefore all the disciples of Christ, persevering in prayer and praising God (cf. Acts 2, 42–7), should present themselves as a living sacrifice, holy and pleasing to God (cf. Rom. 12, 1). Everywhere on earth they must bear witness to Christ and give an answer to those who seek an account of that hope of eternal life which is in them (cf. 1 Pet. 3, 15).

This text is of capital importance because it restores the value of the royal priesthood of the People of God, buried for too long in obscurity by our classical theology. But what is said of the People of God as a whole obviously holds good, proportionately, for every individual member. It signifies the fact that every baptized member shares in the unique priesthood of Christ, priest, prophet and king. The baptized person has indeed a *sacerdotal*

---

[2] The translation used is that of *The Documents of Vatican II*, ed. by W. M. Abbott (London, 1966).

function because he must render worship to the Father; a *prophetic* function because he must spread the message of salvation, and a *royal* function because he must contribute to the establishment of the reign of love in the world. These three points are developed in nn. 11, 12 and 13. The baptized has access to the forms of sacramental life which unite him to God at the various stages of his life on earth. Again, as baptized, he is endowed with a sense of faith and so shares in that *sensus fidelium* that is distributed throughout the People of God and is a *locus theologicus* of truth; here this means that the faithful cannot err as a community when, by universal consent, they affirm a doctrinal point of faith or morals, because they are assisted by the Spirit. The baptized can also receive the charisms of the Spirit for the renewal and development of the Church. Finally, he shares in the expansion of the Church to the end of the world for the gathering of all mankind into unity.

The same basic ideas are recalled in the *Decree on the Apostolate of the Laity,* particularly in nn. 3 and 4. Here again I limit myself to one quotation full of references to Scripture:

> For the exercise of this apostolate, the Holy Spirit who sanctifies the People of God through the ministry and the sacraments gives the faithful special gifts as well (cf. 1 Cor. 12, 7), "allotting to everyone according as he will" (1 Cor. 12, 11). Thus may the individual, "according to the gift that each has received, administer it to one another" and become "good stewards of the manifold grace of God" (1 Pet. 4, 10), and build up thereby the whole body in charity (cf. Eph. 4, 16). From the reception of these charisms or gifts, including those which are less dramatic, there arise for each believer the right and duty to use them in the Church and in the world for the good of mankind and for the upbuilding of the Church. In so doing, believers need to enjoy the freedom of the Holy Spirit who "breathes where he will" (Jn. 3, 8). At the same time, they must act in communion with their brothers in Christ, especially with their pastors.

By restoring this "royal priesthood" the Council could at last recognize and bring out to the full the authentic function of the laity in the Church, a function that is genuinely active and no longer purely passive and subordinate; a specific function and no longer a feeble imitation of the priestly function. The laity have to sanctify the secular world to which they belong through the concrete situation which they occupy there; that is, their vocation and their spirituality—"a continuous exercise of faith, hope and charity"—is given a special character from this and is, so to speak, colored by it.

From these quotations, which could be multiplied, we can draw the following conclusion.[3] The prerogatives of the baptized, deriving from his royal priesthood (and therefore outside any imposition of hands) reach him in a straight line from Christ through the apostolic Church which is priestly in her totality. Here we can distinguish first of all a *gift of apostolic faith,* the too often forgotten condition of any valid ministry as I shall explain further on in greater detail; then there is the fact that "through special gifts of the Spirit" the layman is *enabled* to exercise the apostolate of witness and to render a "spiritual worship" (Rom. 12, 1). Now, all this belongs to the components of the apostolic succession, whether on the part of the material element (the heritage of faith) or on the part of the formal element (the enabling to witness and to render worship). Although this does not constitute the whole of the matter, because Catholic teaching does not allow a layman to celebrate the eucharist, even by delegation, these prerogatives nevertheless constitute an essential part of the succession since they ensure that the baptized are "of" the Church, and better still, are *the* Church: "Christ has made us a kingdom, priests to his God and Father . . . a kingdom and priests to our God and they shall reign on earth" (Apoc. 1, 6 and 5, 9–10). When, therefore, we speak of the ministerial priesthood in the strict sense (bishop and priest) we can only think of it in terms of the ecclesial priesthood and from within this ecclesial priesthood, in other words, within an apostolic succession that benefits the whole People of God.

[3] I refer here to the adult Christian layman, fully conscious of his role in the Church, as is the sense in the conciliar document.

2. *From the Point of View of the Other Churches*

The second group of conciliar texts concerns the ecclesial communities that have sprung from the Reformation, precisely those in which our usual teaching was hardly interested and dealt with, so to speak, *en passant*. Following men whom the institutional Church had rejected, these communities rejected the institutional Church in turn and so could not use an imposition of hands that would place them in the direct line of apostolic succession. We find these texts in chapters I and III of the *Decree on Ecumenism*.

> Moreover some, even very many, of the most significant elements or endowments which together go to build up and give life to the Church herself can exist outside the visible boundaries of the Catholic Church: the written Word of God; the life of grace; faith, hope, and charity, along with other interior gifts of the Holy Spirit and visible elements. All of these, which come from Christ and lead back to him, belong by right to the one Church of Christ.
>
> The brethren divided from us also carry out many of the sacred actions of the Christian religion. Undoubtedly, in ways that vary according to the condition of each Church or Community, these actions can truly engender a life of grace, and can rightly be described as capable of providing access to the community of salvation.
>
> It follows that these separated Churches and Communities, though we believe they suffer from defects already mentioned, have by no means been deprived of significance and importance in the mystery of salvation. For the Spirit of Christ has not refrained from using them as means of salvation which derive their efficacy from the very fullness of grace and truth entrusted to the Catholic Church (n. 3).

It would seem necessary, in our opinion, to read these paragraphs at two different levels, one referring to Churches that have maintained a "Catholic" style and claim both apostolic succession and hierarchical institution, such as the Orthodox Church, the Anglican Church and the Swedish Lutheran Church, the last two creating particular problems, as is known; the other referring to the Churches and Communities of a Protestant character, having rejected both the apostolic succession and the hierarchical institution. It is obvious that the ideas expressed in the conciliar text have not the same implications at both levels. In this article I concentrate only on the second category and I have the impression that these paragraphs apply especially to them, which is promising from the ecumenical point of view. Three conclusions can be drawn:

1. The Roman Catholic Church, as a juridical institution, is not the whole Church. Beyond her visible boundaries she recognizes that Christ grants these Protestant Churches "elements" and "benefits" that are "numerous and of great value", both inward and outward, and which also contribute to the building up and enlivening of the authentic Church.

2. The "sacred acts" of these Churches and Communities can effectively produce a life of grace, which implies a certain sacramental structure (real and not merely the equivalent of it).

3. The Spirit uses these Churches and Communities in order to lead their faithful to salvation.

There is no exaggeration in saying that the meaning of these texts shows the beginning of a recognition of these Churches and Communities *as such*. And which theologian would have dared put these things calmly into writing at the time of the encyclical *Mystici Corporis*? We have something new here, not only in the attitude of the Church of Rome, but in her very theology, in that it has taken on an ecumenical dimension. If, indeed, as all commentators have observed, the *Decree on Ecumenism* has adopted an ecclesiology of *communion* (the future structure of which is not yet clearly understood) must we not begin by recognizing in some degree the partners of this communion, and even starting a dialogue with them on an equal footing?

Chapter III, nn. 20–3, confirms this assumption when it outlines (too briefly, so it seems to me) the list of integrated "values". This list comprises the belief in Christ (God, Lord and the one Mediator, source and center of all ecclesial communion); the love and veneration of Sacred Scripture; the sacramental life (baptism, the sacramental bond of unity, the eucharist, in some incomplete but real way: if these Communities "have not preserved the genuine and total reality" [4] they have preserved something); the life in Christ, and so on. Must all this not be called "apostolic tradition" or "apostolic succession" insofar as the doctrinal and moral content is concerned? And let us not forget that the text is speaking, not at the level of the simple believer, but at that of attributes of Churches.

This leads us to the key question of this article: Where does this solid ecclesial fund come from? Is it enough to refer to the royal priesthood of the People of God as a number of Protestant theologians seem to do in their relentless opposition to a ministerial priesthood which they think they see in our Church as a straight copy of the priesthood of Christ? Or must we refer to the sacramental efficacy of their imposition of hands (more precisely: as an enabling by divine right)? Now, this rite creates a problem for us since it does not fit into our hierarchical descent. We touch here a complex of difficulties that affect both our own theology and that of our Protestant brethren, and which is the most tender point in our dialogue.

We must therefore go farther. We must examine this delicate point with all the questions it poses, and since our theology is not yet ready for any definite solutions, we can at least try to suggest some approaches.

II

PROBLEMS AND SUGGESTIONS

1. Toward a Better Understanding of Apostolic Succession

First of all, we must correct our too simplistic notion of an apostolic succession transmitted by imposition of hands in a purely juridical and formal manner. This notion, which has figured for such a long time in our textbooks, does not correspond

---

[4] Cf. the translation by Card. Bea, Le chemin de l'Unité (Paris, 1967), p. 61.

to that of either the primitive or the medieval tradition of the Church, as Yves Congar has shown in a recent article.[5]

In an *Excursus,* going back to the First Letter of Clement and proceeding to Irenaeus, Gregory the Great, Anselm and Thomas Aquinas, this author traces a very different trend of thought: the formal and juridical legitimacy of a ministry depends *"on a certain content in which conformity with the faith of the apostles occupies the first place"*; in other words, "the apostolicity of the ministry demands apostolicity of doctrine". The faith, the call of Christ, the conferring of a charisma of the Spirit for the service of the community—all these things are the preliminary conditions for the effectiveness of the rite of imposition of hands. Before we speak about "ministries" we should speak of "ministers", i.e., men prepared by the Spirit, and that is why in the practice of the primitive Church the People had a voice in proclaiming the worthiness of the candidate. It follows also that the action of an *episcopus vagrans* (wandering bishop) ordaining more or less without reference to the community is nonsense.

This traditional view began to be obscured from Gregory VII on who is known to have pushed the process of the juridical mentality. This can be seen from the following quotation from the *Dictatus Papae*: "By the fact of his canonical ordination, the Roman pontiff is undoubtedly sanctified through the merits of Blessed Peter." [6] During the centuries-long crisis that followed, when the Spiritualists, Wycliffe, Huss and so many others raised the question of how authentic was the authority of Churchmen who did not live like the apostles, this same juridical tendency grew even stronger and finally crystallized in the idea of a juridical apostolic succession that guaranteed the apostolicity of the faith. And so the original and traditional view was completely reversed. The break of the Reformation in the 16th century could only stiffen the Church's defensive reaction, the

[5] Yves Congar, "Apostolicité de ministère et apostolicité de doctrine, réaction protestante et tradition catholique," in *Volk Gottes. Festgabe für Josef Höfer* (Herder 1967), pp. 84–110.

[6] "Quod Romanus Pontifex, si canonice fuerit ordinatus, meritis beati Petri indubitanter efficitur sanctus" (Congar, *op. cit.,* p. 104).

result of a long traumatism that lasted up to our own time. And now we have Vatican II, stirred by the new spirit of the ecumenical age, restoring a theology of values and looking at all the convergent factors which will, by the grace of God, lead one day to that ecclesiology of communion the main lines of which are still blurred. The re-thinking of the apostolic succession on the lines I have indicated is one of the principal tasks in this immense program. It is important here to give first place to that apostolicity of doctrine in which the Protestant Churches share in spite of limitations and ambiguities. Then we should look carefully at all the factors that might justify the apostolicity of ministry in those Churches.

2. *The Apostolicity of Ministry in the Protestant Churches*

The words "apostolicity of ministry" do not have the same meaning for Catholics and Protestants, and there lies the greatest and apparently insurmountable obstacle. It is hardly necessary to say that on the Catholic side these words imply a *ministerial priesthood,* conferred by imposition of hands in the hierarchical descent of the successors of the apostles. On the Protestant side this line of transmission as well as the results of it is rejected. Perhaps we can try to understand this position.

Rejected by the institutional Church, Luther and the other Reformers took refuge in a *charismatic* structure of the Church for which they thought the communities founded by St. Paul provided the pattern. In this perspective, justified in their eyes by the texts where the apostle speaks of the charisms (Rom. 12, 1 Cor. 12 and Eph. 4), *the whole community of the faithful,* or rather, *the whole Church,* is apostolic and creates its ministers through people moved by the Spirit and faithful to that Word which alone builds up the Church, and it is once again the community as a whole that must judge the faithfulness of these ministers. To limit the apostolic succession to some hierarchs or to some Sees would mean to put a limit on the sovereign independence of the Spirit and the Word. Here we might usefully recall Calvin's aphorism: "The Church is there where the Word of God is preached and listened to in its purity and where the sacraments are rightly administered." The charismatic ministries are merely "the main joints of the body in the exercise of the royal priesthood": they are major signs, points where the succession is manifest, but all the faithful share in it. In these conditions the imposition of hands represents an action of the whole Church. This was the constant conviction of the Reformers and their disciples. Prof. Jean Bosc makes this clear in his comments on the *Constitution on the Church,* from which I have borrowed several of the above statements.[7] One can understand that this position of the Protestants was strongly influenced by the urgency of the situation in which they found themselves, but, for all that, it is not less founded on a definite view of the New Testament. The Protestant commentator is therefore happy to see some traces of this view in chapter II of the Constitution. The tension persists nevertheless with regard to the ministerial priesthood, presented in the Constitution as *essentially* distinct from the royal priesthood.[8]

One might think, then, that the ordination to pastoral service has but a minor importance in the mind of the Protestant Churches. That, however, is not true and we should realize, on the contrary, how seriously it has always been taken, even in the liberal milieus of the 19th and 20th centuries, as represented by Alexander Vinet or Wilfred Monod, for instance. And we should not forget that Calvin, rather more constructive than Luther, gave it the value of a sacrament—the third sacrament— which confers special gifts of the Spirit in view of the ministries, the power of which derived from the royal priesthood.[9]

[7] J. Bosc, "La Constitution dogmatique *Lumen Gentium,*" in *Vatican II, points de vue de théologiens protestants* (Paris, 1967), pp. 15–46, esp. 32. This commentary bringing out either points of convergence or reactions against, is a model of ecumenical penetration.

[8] On this major difficulty concerning "the nature of the ministry" (J. Bosc) see note 15 below.

[9] L. Schummer, *Le ministère pastoral dans l'Institution chrétienne de Calvin à la lumière du troisième sacrement* (Wiesbaden, 1965), esp. the 2nd part, the pastoral ministry in the light of the third sacrament, 36–95 and theses 95–6. This interpretation of Calvin, which seems to be the most authentic, is gaining support among Protestant theologians. It should

Could we, aware of present-day ecumenical pressures, ask a question by way of conclusion to this section? Could the Catholic Church not accept the idea of a form of ministry, not integrated in the apostolic succession, or, in other words, outside the chain of the imposition of hands in the line of hierarchical descent?

3. *The Ministry of the Word*

Avery Dulles, S.J., has concentrated on this difficult problem in his doctoral thesis, *Protestant Churches and the Prophetic Office,*[10] defended at the Gregorian University in 1960, and one can imagine that in this perilous pursuit he has used the most meticulous caution. His research was limited to the ministry of the Word, taken as primary in Protestant teaching. This ministry demands a "prophetic mission" to acquire authenticity. The priest receives this mission at his ordination through the necessary hierarchical channel. But could this mission not pass through another channel? Are the remarkable results of Protestant preaching—so often considered to be better than Catholic preaching—not a pointer in favor of an authentic mission?

To refuse to answer the question is mere escapism.[11] To assimilate the pastor to a simple layman bearing witness to his faith, or to say that his sermon is effective only because of the sources

---

help us as Catholics to bring more precision to the conditions required for a recognition of the Protestant ministries. If Calvin, who supported the sacrament of orders, refused to accept the ministerial priesthood, the reason seems to be that contemporary Catholic theology wrongly stressed the Mass as a "repetition" of the sacrifice of the cross. But there is kind of equivalence in his position. The pastor is successor to the apostles for life. The pastoral ministry fits into the framework of an "embassy" of reconciliation and represents Christ's priesthood. There is, in Calvin, a priesthood of "embassy". Its relation to Christ's priesthood is neither that of succession, nor that of an innovation, but one of delegation or representation. The power is attributed to the *function* not to the *person*. These points, which carry complementary aspects, could be useful topics for discussion in a dialogue.

[10] A. Dulles, *Protestant Churches and the Prophetic Office* (Woodstock Coll. Press, 1961). I only give a brief outline of this thesis which abounds in new points of view.

[11] This was the wholly negative reply given by P. Charles in "Réflexions sur la théologie du sermon. Prédication et Prédicateurs," in *Nouv. Rev. Théol.* (1947), pp. 25–48.

he makes use of (Scripture, the Fathers and Doctors, and even the Catholic magisterium), is simply to make light of what we ourselves accept as the greatest values. We are right in believing that such a pastor acts in obedience to a genuine call, sanctioned by an authentic charism. How could the action of the Spirit be tied down to a juridical body? And we have to admit that this action of the Spirit extends well beyond this body, although, we believe, always in reference to the universal Church. And so the dissident prophet, whose good faith is beyond doubt, can receive a true mission by means of a charism.[12] It is indeed remarkable that the great Protestant "revivals" are always marked by ecumenical re-discoveries, and often in the "Catholic" sense.[13]

But there is more. One has to reckon with the rite of the imposition of hands, although received outside the hierarchical descent.[14] No doubt, we cannot take it as "valid". But does this mean that it lacks efficacy? Fr. Dulles thinks—and I agree with him—that it is a "vestige of the Church" in the prophetic line and that it carries with it grace for the building up of the Church, although there is a certain ambiguity. It is the recognition of an inward charism; it bestows on the candidate a public quality before the community: the pastor is a "sacred person", not merely as an individual, but as president of the liturgical function. Although without the power of orders and jurisdiction, he is nevertheless given a *function* of preaching and he receives a gift of grace in order to lead his flock to the truth. It is not as if God wanted dissidence, but, given this dissidence, God does not abandon his People. If one will not grant that Calvin's Protestant ordination is a true sacrament (he himself would not

---

[12] A. Dulles, *op. cit.,* "Protestant ministries: The Charismatic Aspect," pp. 27f. Cf. M. Villain and J. de Baciocchi, *La vocation de l'Eglise* (Paris, 1954), p. 222.

[13] Following L. Bouyer, Fr. Dulles shows the prophetic role of men like Wesley, Kierkegaard, Gruntvig, Adolphe Monod and K. Barth to the advantage of "Catholic" values: transcendence, divinity of Christ, rejection of modernism, etc. *Ibid.,* p. 32.

[14] A. Dulles, *ibid.,* pp. 33f., "Protestant Ministries: Institutional Aspects."

accept an action *ex opere operato*), one may nevertheless suggest with Fr. Dulles that it is a share (a quasi-sacrament) insofar as it is a "confession of faith in the power of Christ's passion and a fervent prayer to obtain the grace in order to fulfill the ministry in a manner pleasing to God". And in the degree that the candidate would have the *votum sacramenti* (the wish to receive the sacrament, of which God alone can judge), he would receive the *res sacramenti* (the reality of the sacrament). Consequently, by sanctioning a charismatic vocation the Protestant ordination would add a grace of ministry to the baptismal priesthood.

4. *The Ministry of the Sacraments*

There remains the peculiarly delicate topic of the enabling of a person to exercise a sacramental function of which the central action is the celebration of the eucharist. The thesis I have referred to does not touch on this burning issue but at the point where we have arrived in our discussion and particularly in the climate of the post-conciliar discussions where the problem of intercommunion has moved into the foreground, we cannot afford to neglect this further stage in our pursuit.

The Catholic view strictly insists that the ministerial priesthood must be acquired by means of the hierarchy, and the same holds for the Orthodox. For lack of this, the minister of a Presbyterian Church cannot celebrate the eucharist validly. But, however absolute this negative verdict may be, it does not exhaust the subject because, by formulating the problem in this way, one is in danger of forgetting that such "Presbyterian" Communities have preserved, as such, a certain part of the reality of the eucharistic mystery, as shown by the text of the *Decree on Ecumenism,* quoted above. Those words imply more than a souvenir or a mere symbol. We have here a value that cannot be assessed in juridical terms and that a sound ecumenical theology cannot let go to waste. Moreover, the minister is intimately convinced of having this power, thought out in terms of an approach that differs from ours, and he refers to the reasons, given above, in order to justify the prophetic ministry. Can we say that these reasons are meaningless here?

If Protestant doctrine holds that the power to celebrate the sacrament is radically included in the royal priesthood, it also holds that only he can use it who can make good his claim that he has received a call from Christ and a special charism from the Spirit, sanctioned by the imposition of hands by the consecrating ministers. Through the concept of collegiality these ministers represent the whole Church as the bearer of the apostolic succession, and in the same liturgical formula they testify, on behalf of the Church, that the enabling power is granted by God to the candidate in respect of the dispensation of both the Word *and* the sacraments. According to Calvin, the Holy Spirit confers the gifts appropriate to this double function and added to the royal priesthood.[15] To pretend, as some more radical Protestant authors do, that the pastor is nothing but a layman employed full-time for the service of the Church is an opinion that is considered erroneous and harmful by the better theologians.

As to the biblical foundation of that conviction, we are asked to look for it in the Epistles of St. Paul. It is a fact that the Churches founded by Paul do not show the same structure as that of Jerusalem, the heir to the College of Twelve, presided over by Peter, and it would appear that "the right hand of fellowship" offered by James, Cephas and John to Paul and Barnabas (Gal. 2, 9) did not make the slightest difference. The doctrine of the charismatic ministries (i.e., conferred by the Spirit for the building up of the body of Christ) does not give the impression of a different mode of access to either one or the other type of ministry (apostle, doctor, pastor). What stands out, above all, is the free operation of the Spirit, and it is not *evident* that the

---

[15] Here we have a very important point of convergence in the major difficulty about the "ministerial priesthood". I know disciples of Calvin who would subscribe to the following sentence: "Within the ecclesial priesthood the Holy Spirit chooses himself 'ministers' who, through their ordination, are enabled to minister pastorally (Word and sacraments) by special gifts." This could be the equivalent of the ministerial priesthood, although the word "minister" is substituted for "priest," considered non-biblical.

succession passes, *of absolute necessity*, through the founding apostle rather than through the college of presbyters. Who celebrated the eucharist at Corinth when Paul sent them his first letter, not in order to correct an error in the presidency but moral abuses? From the point of view of exegesis, the question remains open; so does that of the presidency of the college of presbyters at Ephesus, in which Calvin saw the prototype of the presbyteral college for his reform. In short, the Protestant exegete is of the opinion that the Churches of Paul developed along a presbyteral line, while the community of Jerusalem followed another line, more episcopal and Judaic, before the development took place which, after passing through the stage of the pastoral epistles, led to the mono-episcopacy of Asia Minor after the death of the apostles.

There is no need to discuss this extraordinarily difficult problem here.[16] All I want to show is the coherence of the position of the presbyteral Churches in the state where a solution was urgent and where they have maintained themselves for centuries. It also shows how the pastors vindicate their conviction.[17] It is clear that the drafters of the *Decree on Ecumenism* have taken note of it, and that is why, beyond the restoration of the value of the royal priesthood by the *Constitution on the Church*, they insisted on bringing out, without giving the source of their statement, the eucharistic values that can be preserved through an imposition of hands other than along our hierarchical line. Although our Protestant brethren are not satisfied with that, they are grateful for this modest concession as a clear sign of progress. In return, we are convinced that the Catholic thesis of the ministerial priesthood, purged from the wrong meaning

---

[16] The Protestant is not susceptible to our Catholic concept of a homogeneous development. Even when admitting that it is particularly well-founded historically in this case (M. Thurian, "L'organization du ministère dans l'Eglise primitive selon saint Ignace d'Antioche," in *Verbum Caro*, 81) he would still ask us to admit that there is an interval of a dual structure in the New Testament.

[17] As a borderline case, a "catholicizing" pastor, haunted by the idea of the ministerial priesthood, would normally think that he possessed this priesthood by way of a charism. The case is not wholly imaginary.

with which it was encumbered in the past, may now be better understood by them. Some would be prepared to accept it as a normal development along the "Petrine" line on condition that another development along the "Pauline" line was equally accepted. What theologians like J. L. Leuba, J. J. von Allmen and Max Thurian would like to see is the recognition by the Catholic Church of the *diversity* in the forms of the ministry.

Conclusion

As I said at the beginning, the second part of this article has, above all, led to questions that ultimately converge on this one: Will the Catholic Church ever recognize the ministries of the Churches born of the Reformation, so that this recognition may be the prelude to that (bilateral) intercommunion so much longed for today? As we have seen, these questions are not yet ripe, but it is already genuine progress that we can broach them in a spirit of serenity and keep them open.

We need not despair. Christ said to his apostles: "I appointed you" (I have established my Church definitively). Schisms, of whatever kind, do not decide everything. This conviction, which lay at the heart of the primitive Church, is coming to life again in this ecumenical age, in the conscience of all Christian denominations, with or without apostolic succession (in the general sense of the word). It has remained very much alive in the Protestant Churches that see themselves as constantly re-created by the Word and the profession of faith in "Christ the Son of the living God". In spite of their congenital weaknesses they feel themselves as part of the universal Church. The World Council of Churches has its anchor in this same conviction (did its pioneers not see themselves as carrying on the Reformation of the 16th century?). And, finally, Vatican II re-discovered this intuition when it looked again at the mystery of the "People of God" which a too juridical defensive and aggressive attitude tended to overlook. What would the *Decree on Ecumenism* be without this conviction which is assumed throughout and which leads it to a new perspective of "communion"? And now that we have begun to assimilate it, who would dare maintain that the fruits of preaching, of eucharistic understanding and of sanctity among our Protestant brethren are but something marginally equivalent to grace? The marvel of Taizé, to quote but one universally known case, would plainly contradict such an assertion. Let us say it frankly: those fruits mature within the universal Church; they spring from that "sacramental" character which is mysterious by definition, always alive and always operative. The day will come, we hope, when, with the help of adequate guarantees of the traditional doctrine on the *mysterium fidei* and all opposition to the apostolic succession having ceased, the proper consistency of the eucharist among our Protestant brethren will be recognized—in virtue of the principle of *Ecclesia supplet* or of "economy" in Orthodox terminology, *even if the principle would have to be extended to situations where it has as yet never been applied.*[18] For the Church, mistress of the sacraments, can decide thus.[19] The Protestant communities would then have to accept this sign of communion in order to mend the schisms. On that day the internal bond that has always existed in Christ will be made manifest in the fullness of light.

[18] The question of *Ecclesia supplet* or "economy" is beyond the scope of this study. See, however, Archimandrite Pierre, "Economie ecclésiastique dans la théologie orthodoxe," in *Irénikon* (1937), pp. 228–47 and 339–62; A. Alivisatos, " 'Economy' from the Orthodox Point of View," in *Dispensation in Practice and Theory* (London, 1944), pp. 27f.; Y. Congar, "Economie" in *Catholicisme*. I deliberately stress the conditions in which "economy" could operate in favor of the Protestant ministries, even though it would be a new concession made for the sake of progress in unity.

[19] This is held by both Orthodox and Catholics.

Joseph Duss-von Werdt/*Zurich, Switzerland*

What Can the Layman Do without the Priest?

Within the scope of the general theme of this volume, the question here raised is likewise concerned with succession: the succession, not of the ministry, transmitted by imposition of hands in the Church, but of the Church herself, understood as the community of those who believe, hope and love. How does the Church continue, express and realize herself, if there is no "priest", or better, no one appointed by imposition of hands to preside over the community? The fact *that* she endures—visibly, too—follows from the theological statements about the laity, more particularly about the "universal priesthood". The way in which she endures, on the other hand, raises complex and delicate problems. They amount to a demand for theology to reflect on what is the real content and meaning of the universal priesthood. This contribution is intended solely to raise certain aspects of this question (which is already difficult enough), not to answer it.

1. *The Metacanonical Starting Point*

We would be taking the question too easily, with its legal undertones, if we were to start out unquestioningly from the prevailing law and the present order of "states" in the Church, which it presupposes, as the normal order and then merely ask: "Can (that is, may) the layman preach, administer sacraments (which?), and so on?" Legal demarcations are necessary in the first place for reasons of Church discipline. But the law, too, must be substantiated from a metacanonical, "basic" sphere. "Basic" means: rooted in the origin, as it is attested in the original documents of the faith, the Old and New Testaments.

What form did the structures of the first communities take? Who assumed in them the communal (liturgical, kerygmatic, pastoral) functions? Here, too, there is not an adequate starting point in an ecclesiology that does not prove itself as the "dominant whence" at the origin of which we spoke. The relevance of a radical questioning is evident today in connection with the renewal of the diaconate (what can the deacon alone do, but not the layman?); it is however particularly acute where the Church is in extreme need (concentration camps, persecution, shortage of priests, missions, etc.), where it may be a question of the Church's survival. Nevertheless, even for borderline situations, merely *ad hoc* solutions cannot be adopted. Every solution must be right in principle.[1]

2. *Open Questions of Exegesis*

However, it is by no means easy to throw light on origins. The biblical evidence suggests a variety of community orders and therefore the hermeneutic value of passages indicating a tradition of uniformity becomes a problem. Here we are restricting ourselves to questions of exegesis.

Difficulties begin already when we attempt to understand our theme in the light of the origins. What the layman can do without the priest or, positively, what the priest alone can do, cannot be answered in biblical terms. From the biblical standpoint, then, who is a "layman" and who a "priest"?[2] When were the apostles "ordained priests" (they are never called such)? If we want to speak of lay people (the word is unknown to the New Testa-

---

[1] For the diaconate, cf. K. Rahner, H. Vorgrimler, J. Kramer, "Zur Erneuerung des Diakonats in Deutschland," in *Stimmen der Zeit,* 180 (1967), pp. 145–153.

[2] On this see H. Küng, *Die Kirche* (Freiburg im Breisgau, 1967) pp. 152f. and 439f. I have relied largely on this work, especially on the exegetical conclusions set out there.

ment) even to a slight degree in accordance with the Bible, then we can only say that they are those who belong to the People of God (λαὸς θεοῦ).[3]

In their totality they are called *"priesthood"* (1 Pet. 2, 9), "saints" (Paul). The answer to our question, therefore, depends decisively on how much we invest in this "universal priesthood" and in the "priestliness" of all. There is no mention in the New Testament of a "special" priesthood within the communities: the ministers of the community in the New Testament are deliberately never called "priests". If, nevertheless, there is to be a legitimate, special ministry to the community, it will then in any case exist only within the scope of the universal priesthood: there is no other priesthood by contrast to this, but we can see in the universal priesthood a particular formation or, as will become clear, formations.

In the undisputed Pauline epistles it is impossible to establish any reference to an ordination. Nor can it, on that account, simply be tacitly presupposed. *Everyone can do that to which he has been called, that which has been given him through the charism.* The charism stems neither from the community (even though it is to be accepted and confirmed by the latter) nor from an "office" existing for its own sake apart from the charisms.[4] It is the *basic category* of the Pauline community-order and co-extensive with ministry (charismatic order = diaconal structure).

It is different in the pastoral epistles. Like the Acts of the Apostles, these are aware of ordination by imposition of hands; we cannot, however, go on at once to assert that its modern form and content were thus established.[5] Timothy was indeed ordained

---

[3] F. Wulf, "Ueber die Herkunft und den ursprünglichen Sinn des Wortes Laie," *Geist und Leban,* 32 (1959), pp. 61–63; J. Duss-von Werdt, "Der Laie in der nachkonziliaren Kirche," in *Schweizer Rundschau,* 7 (1966), pp. 397–407.

[4] H. Küng, "The Charismatic Structure of the Church," in *Concilium,* Vol. 4: *The Church and Ecumenism* (Glen Rock: Paulist Press, 1965) pp. 41–61.

[5] Are these not also the result of a "sacralizing process" emerging with the aid of sociological categories of "clergy"—"laity" (cf. F. X. Arnold, "Laie", in *Wörterbuch der Politik* [Freiburg im Breisgau, 1960], pp. 209f.) and both religious—but unscriptural—and sacral-profane ideas, or in con-

by the elders, "when they laid their hands upon [him]", but in virtue of "a prophetic utterance" (1 Tim. 4, 14). As distinct from (or as complementing) 2 Timothy 1, 6, in which is mentioned "the gift of God . . . through the laying on of my hands", the charism already known was therefore here acknowledged and confirmed and not mediated in virtue of imposition of hands. Here, too, is at least a hint of the objective and *temporal* priority of the charism. From the general charismatic community-order (together with Paul; cf. also 1 Pet. 4, 10) the gifts of grace do not come only to a particular group of persons; each has his charism. Nor is there any evidence that ordination set up classes with precisely definable spheres of exercise. Every charism more-over has its own "authority", not as a result of horizontal media-tion, but based on vocation by the Spirit: it exists not because of the office, but because of the Spirit (1 Cor. 12, 11).

The extent and content of what is involved in a charism can-not be clearly determined. We cannot, for example, determine whether only a person endowed with the gift of leading (1 Cor. 12, 28) presided at the eucharistic meal and not also an "apos-tle", "teacher" or "prophet". In other words: the inexchange-ability of the charisms (each has precisely *his own*) is far from implying that particular ecclesial (liturgical, pastoral, etc.) func-tions are linked inexchangeably and irrecusably to particular charisms, or conversely, that particular charisms are, so to speak, "automatically" involved in a special ecclesial function.

Furthermore: if one of the "organizational forms" of com-munity was the house-community (not as a private family-com-munity, but as a meeting point for Christians of different fami-lies), then according to the Pauline community-order it must be assumed that from time to time the head of the household also presided at it. Anyone wanting to assert that this person was al-ways an ordained priest would be taking on himself a burden of proof very hard to bear in the light of the Pauline epistles. Even if more distinctions must be made than is possible here, from

nection with 1 Corinthians 2, 14 and the expressions, "worldly" (fleshly) —"spiritual" (pneumatic)?

the standpoint of exegesis the conclusion must be drawn: the earliest, the apostolic Church, is aware of several possible community orders, at least of those with and those without ordained persons.

If the original, the apostolic Church, is the "dominant whence" for the subsequent Church (and scarcely anyone will dispute this), the latter also must in principle be open to several possibilities, at least to those attested in Scripture; it must allow pluralism to prevail and not, for instance, use violence to bring the charismatic Corinthian Church under a common denominator with the more institutionalized Church of the pastoral epistles. Certainly Paul cannot be excluded from the Corinthian Church. The First Epistle to the Corinthians shows clearly enough how much he made his authority as "apostle" (*his* charism) prevail. Nevertheless, in view of 1 Corinthians 11, 17–34, it cannot be assumed that in Corinth during his absence the eucharist was dropped any more than preaching was dropped. Who presided? We know nothing about anyone being specially ordained: neither in connection with preaching nor in connection with the eucharist (cf. also the Didache where prophets are still described as directing the eucharist).

3. *Charisms as Particularizations of the Universal Priesthood*

Any discussion of the "universal priesthood" must rely mainly on 1 Peter 2, 9, an epistle which, from the historical standpoint is in the Pauline tradition. Objectively, this "Petrine" manner of speaking coincides primarily with the Pauline, when Paul speaks of the "saints" (cf. the opening addresses of the epistles) and "pneumatics". All this justifies the Pauline interpretation of the "Petrine" theme, which will be attempted in the following summary of the exegetical evidence.

(a) A distinction must be made between charisms belonging to the individual (the criterion of their genuineness being their contribution to the building up of the whole) on the one hand and specially instituted ecclesial ministries on the other. The former are "inspirations", operations of the Spirit; the latter can be transmitted in and by the community (as when someone is called to the episcopate by the community, a fact attested, for example, in post-apostolic times), the appointed ministers being assigned a special role.

(b) Universal priesthood does not mean that everyone can do everything (1 Cor. 12, 29: "Are all apostles . . . teachers . . . ?"), that in the abstract everyone is equal to everyone else. What is contained in his charism is what establishes for the individual the priestly ministry possible to *him*. All charisms do in fact betoken priestly ministries, but their multiplicity implies their particularization and unfolding. The priestly factor must not be tied, as in the Old Testament, to sacrifice and cult. Multiplicity of charisms means that the individual can do only what is given him to do. His gift is a fragment in the whole, and probably the whole itself is merely a fragment. Multiplicity however is distinction and interdependence through mutual indigence; it is imperfection and provisionality. The multifariousness of the gifts of grace itself is the result of a "state of emergency". To admit this is to escape the danger of a "charismatic unrealism".

(c) Comparison of the different charisms (= ministries), making all due allowance for the precedence of the apostles, cannot produce biblical evidence for an ultimately decisive sub- and super-ordination. The real super-ordinate is the *one* Spirit who works all in everyone (1 Cor. 12, 6). Precedence among Christians under the one Spirit is held, not by individuals (for instance, the "leader" or the "teacher"), but by the *one* body, into which all are baptized (1 Cor. 12, 13). Is not the "monarchical episcopate" therefore merely *one* (possible) interpretation of community order? Is there "office" in fullness and otherwise only "participation" in it?

(d) *Each* has his gift (1 Cor. 12, 7; Eph. 4, 16), in order to work with it on the building up of the *one* body. The universal priesthood betokens this basic charismatic state of every member of the community of Christ.[6] Nor is it abandoned by the person

[6] Speaking from the standpoint of the idea of the People of God: since all form this People, there are no "laymen" within it who would be the "People" in contrast to a ruling group as the "not-People".

who attains to supreme functions of government in the Church. Any distinction of the various ministries within the whole is therefore secondary and relative. Ministry is such only when it is related to the whole. If it turns into the opposite and becomes a claim to power, making the whole subordinate to itself, it no longer serves the whole and is no longer an ecclesial ministry. No ministry is exclusive in such a way as to render the others superfluous. None unites in itself the fullness, the pleroma. The principle of unity is "in the Lord", the pleroma absolutely speaking, whose Spirit "apportions to each individually as he wills" (1 Cor. 12, 11); its realization is in the mutual ministry of all.

(e) As indicated, according to the New Testament, the various ministries are not exclusively tied to particular, institutionalized "offices" and do not exist only in association with these (many a one can preach, because he has the gift, but does not do so, because he has no *officium* for it; for public activity in the community he needs a mandate). The determination of the content of the various ministries and the demarcation of their extent, however, are so difficult to settle from the Bible that we ought to speak only with great caution about "divine law" in relation to episcopal office, priesthood and diaconate. Instead of saying that the Church in the course of time has more and more clearly recognized what belongs to the essence of the ecclesial ministry and its gradation, it would be closer to historical truth to say that she had herself more and more clearly defined this, but that these determinations would have to remain largely within the field of human law (the three-office-order from the time of Ignatius of Antioch).

That an institutionalization, a structure giving a visible organization to the Church, is justified, is not in question; to assert the opposite would be a naive blindness to history and reality. In principle it was a legitimate development, which became marked also in Corinth in post-apostolic times and which led to the more institutionalized community constitution of the Acts of the Apostles and the pastoral epistles and finally to the universally prevailing episcopal-presbyteral order. Nevertheless, charisms cannot be institutionalized. Rather must the Church be intent upon those vocations from the Spirit which cause the institutional element to be "filled with the Spirit".

(f) To return finally to the opening question: It cannot be established *a priori* what the "layman" can do without the "priest". The result of what has been said is rather a shift of emphasis in the question. It is no longer a question of what "the" layman can do, but of what "laymen" (not everyone) can do in the light of the current legal-sociological conception today. "Can" in this respect does not mean mimicry or imitation, but an effective and valid capacity. Presupposing this more exact definition, we can say: in virtue of the universal priesthood, in principle, "laymen" can do everything without "priests".

Again however we must distinguish: "in principle" does not mean that they ought in fact to do so. That would be to claim a right illegitimately, regardless of the necessity of the special mandate for exercising universal priestly functions in the particular public ministry to the community as such, and thus, as a result of unscriptural and historically blind naiveté, would introduce an anarchical element into the order which has come into existence (certainly not entirely out of biblical elements) and persists.

"Everything" does not mean anything quantitative, but must be understood in a qualitative sense: the "priest" is neither mediator of salvation nor exclusive "minister of the fruits of salvation". Christ lives and works through the Spirit in the "layman" just as, and under the same conditions as in the "priests". The "same condition" is that they hear, keep and do his Word in faith, hope and charity.

That the Church continues in this becomes evident. This is not a human achievement, but effected by the Spirit. Man, however, does not decide the conditions of this operation. If the acknowledgment of her direction by the Spirit ceases in the Church, then the Church ceases. From the standpoint of purely legalistic thinking this pneumatological priority is a "dangerous" chaotic element, but for theology and for faith the sole creative and vivifying element.

4. Realizations of the Universal Priesthood

If the above is valid, it involves also the premises for answering particular, concrete questions.[7] Only some of these will be outlined here.

(a) The laity have a share in the whole task of the Church, not only in the derivative or subsidiary sense or through their sympathy (*sentire cum ecclesia?*), but as an essential right. Its fulfillment, however, is not possible in the same way for everyone. But whatever form it takes must be priestly. At the same time it is not a question of worship in a sanctuary, "but of worship in the midst of the world, in the midst of ordinary, secular life: loving devotion to men arising from loving devotion to God and vice-versa".[8]

(b) Christian life takes shape from the Word of God: interpreted by the Word and itself an interpretation of the Word. Living proclamation requires expression in words. Preaching is not its sole form. Literature, theology in studies and teaching, discussions with questioners and seekers, advice to the perplexed, catechesis in all shades—these are forms of proclaiming the Word that can be realized by laymen. What objections of a theological or historical character can be brought against preaching by lay people? Lack of training is not a theological objection. Lay preaching was still possible at the Council of Trent!

(c) It has long been recognized that any Christian can *baptize* —and not only Christians (baptism by heretics!). In contrast to the proclamation of the Word, it requires no charism. In *penance* a distinction would have to be made between forgiveness of sin (in the internal forum) and reconciliation with the community after excommunication through sin. For the latter, the qualified representative of the community is authorized. In the former every Christian can actively cooperate: lay confession has behind it a centuries-old tradition in the history of the Church. What is

---

[7] For a more detailed treatment see H. Küng, *op. cit.,* pp. 440f., 520–522; Y. Congar, *Jalons pour une théologie du laicat* (Paris, 1954), pp. 300–307; (Eng. tr.: *Lay People in the Church* [Westminister: Newman, 1965]).

[8] H. Küng, *op. cit.,* p. 442.

the situation with the *eucharist?* Must a community now consisting solely of lay people be content with Scripture readings and "spiritual communion"? Or must it not be recognized that the charism of leading might dawn on one of them, that they can accept this—at least as "emergency ordination"? The important thing is to remain ready for the free operation of the Spirit, to whom conditions cannot be prescribed by men—not even by an appeal to "divine law".

The real borderline situation and the extreme need of the pilgrim Church at a particular place is not the absence of the "priest", but the disappearance of the faithful, of the universal priesthood, until only one is left. Only then can the Church as such no longer be realized: baptism presupposes a baptizer; the eucharist without a community is an intrinsic contradiction. But as long as the universal priesthood and its charismatic formation are realized, the Church continues, even though the chain of imposition of hands is broken. The biblical key word for our question lies in the promise of what is perhaps the oldest community-order of the primitive Church: "For where two or three are gathered in my name, there am I in the midst of them" (Mt. 18, 20). The important thing is unity in him. Then the Church is reality.

Elizabeth Gössmann / *Munich, W. Germany*

Women as Priests?

Catholic interest in this subject has mushroomed recently and the number and variety of the views expressed have now become so considerable that sorting them out and presenting them critically would achieve little in relation to the effort it would require. I shall therefore approach the matter by asking what concept of hierarchy and what type of practical transformation of ecclesiastical office would be presupposed were it considered appropriate for men and women to work side by side within them. Curiously, this approach has been largely ignored, yet without taking it into consideration the question of the ordination of women frequently causes embarrassment and provokes needless ill-feeling.

I

THE HIERARCHICAL CLASSIFICATION OF REALITY

It has been encouraging to observe that recent official pronouncements have increasingly used the word "hierarchy" in the sense of the duty of service each of us owe to one another. It is a usage, however, that seems to be ahead of the reality. For "hierarchy", both in the sense of ecclesiastical office and as an attitude to life generally (the former having given rise to the latter) used to be something very different from what one might suspect when reading these pronouncements. Consider, for instance, how it has developed in the history of Western thought, particularly as influenced by Neo-Platonism. It was not so much that the notion of service was lacking but rather that in Western thought hierarchy meant first and foremost the immutable relationship of overdog to underdog. This is a manner of thinking with which the new notion of hierarchy has little in common. We are witnessing a change in the meaning behind the word, though not yet a change in the reality. In fact, as we shall see, the actual structures seem once again to be hardening into the old concept of rank and chains of command.

It is no exaggeration to say that in the Christian tradition created beings have always been seen in terms of a descending order of rank. As Augustine put it: "In the first instance God's providence made all things subject to the spiritual order, then the irrational to the rational, the earthly to the heavenly, the woman to the man, the less desirable to the more desirable, the needy to the rich." [1] In other words, everything that exists does so within a hierarchy from which it cannot escape, is senior to some, subordinate to others, and, of course, also has its equals. This order of things is sacred. In his commentary on the Pseudo-Dionysian work *De divinis nominibus,* St. Thomas Aquinas refers to the God-given "grades of existence". [2] Here hierarchy is first defined somewhat vaguely as holy dominion. This ontologically conceived system of mediation from higher to lower grade guarantees world order which, as ordered perfection, mirrors the perfection of the one *causa universalis.* "The peace of God rests upon all things and unites all things through placing them within a particular order. This order consists in the fact that the highest beings are joined to those at the opposite end of the scale through intermediary beings. For the highest beings influence the lowest through intermediaries, and through the intermediaries the lowest beings are connected to the highest according to what they receive." [3]

---

[1] *De genesi ad litt.,* VIII, 23, 44. *P.L.* 34, 390.
[2] Cf., e.g., *op. cit.,* C. V, 1. II; C. IV, 1, I.
[3] *Ibid.,* C. XI, 1, II.

This metaphysically conceived world order would suppose that the relationship of created beings to one another can be considered only in terms of the eventual reduction to the principal cause, the transcendental creator-God, a conception that bridges the gap between the finite and the infinite, and that doing so includes the analogous conception that the God-world relationship is mirrored in every worldly hierarchical relationship, whether one of spirit-matter, human-animal, or man-woman. (Perhaps I should add that in saying this no assault is intended on metaphysical thought as a whole.)

This broad-based, triangular-shaped network of relationships, whose apex was God, served to explain the cosmic order, and eventually took root within the ecclesiological concept of hierarchy, so that this, too, was gripped by the urge to differentiate according to rank. It even got to the point when the mediation of salvation could be viewed in similarly schematic fashion.

So it came about that, with the Christian view of the world firmly established, all legal systems, whether of Church or State, were modelled so as to reflect an all-embracing hierarchical structure within which a man had his superiors and inferiors. Both the Church's constitution and the political order were regulated by a hierarchical outlook people believed to be eternal and immutable, and proper to the nature of man and the rest of creation.

Should one today feel the need to advise against a so-called "democratization" of the Church on the ground that the Church represents a spiritual order above such processes, then one should recall that both civil and ecclesiastical order rest upon a thought system whose historically-conditioned nature can be very precisely determined, but from which the civil order is more readily deflected than the Church's "suprahistorical" and more lasting structures.

Until the onset of modern biblical science people believed that the Bible confirmed the hierarchical conception of created being and the permanency of it as a system to live by. The time was yet to come when it could be seen that though the Bible does not condemn its every aspect, it certainly reflects a very different way of thinking.

But my object here is not simply to discover why, given the subordination of the female sex to the "hierarchically" superior male sex, it took so long in ordinary social life for the notion and realization of partnership to emerge, or to emerge in such limited fashion in the ecclesial sphere. It is significant that, generally speaking, the "hierarchy" of man over woman went undoubted, both in theory and in practice, long after non-hierarchically conceived relationships could be designated as such without first making various reservations. Consider, for instance, how strongly the principle of consultation, and to that extent a "democratic" way of thinking, dominated the thought of men such as Raymund Lull and Nicholas of Cusa alongside the continuing acceptance of the hierarchical thought system, and how difficult it was found to reconcile the two notions.

It should by now be clear that as long as we preserve, whether consciously or unconsciously, a notion of "hierarchy" in terms of graded ranks within created being, as long, in other words, as we insist on thinking of a bishop as somehow "more" than a "simple" layman, rather than someone who exercises a different function, the question of a female ministry is simply a frivolous one offering no realizable goal. However, that the question has nevertheless arisen, and cannot now be suppressed, means that we should probe at least as deep as the answer lies.

II

THE PRESENT STAGE OF THE DISCUSSION

Let us now establish the shape of the discussion within the Catholic Church so that some conclusions can then be drawn in the light of what has been said earlier.[4]

The traditional arguments ranged against the admission of

[4] Cf. particularly R. J. A. van Eyden, "Die Frau im Kirchenamt", in *Wort und Wahrheit,* 22 (1967), pp. 350–62. This source also supplies a wide-ranging bibliography indicating English, Dutch and German language attitudes to this question.

women to ecclesiastical office are these: (1) The twelve apostles were chosen exclusively from male candidates; (2) The man is more suited than the woman to a public role; (3) The affinity between Christ as man and the priest as man; (4) The hierarchical superiority of the male over the female sex.

Those for or against these arguments, and the bodies of opinion each of them represents, take their stand in various ways. Those who oppose the admission of women to ecclesiastical office do so either because (A) the reasons for their exclusion, so far regarded as valid, should remain so, being supratemporal; or (B) it is agreed that these reasons are now outdated and it is argued that in the Church's present situation it would be inopportune if not harmful to raise the barrier.

Those in favor of the admission of women to the priesthood can also be divided into two groups. One group (A) would hope to realize its goal within the existing framework of Church structures, thinking in terms of celibacy and virginity, vocation and status; while the other (B) reckons with the flexibility of the Church's structures and with an extremely radical transformation of ecclesiastical office in the concrete, reckoning also that the potential they see, were the possibilities they have in mind realized, could be readily combined with an image of womanhood that is of "mythical" proportions rather than simply traditional ones, and which, therefore, would hardly be welcomed by contemporary psychology or anthropology.

It will be of value to us to examine these differing viewpoints more closely.

Opponent group A remains unconvinced by H. van der Meer's surely flawless demonstration that the traditional reasons for refusing women admission to the priesthood no longer hold water in this day and age.[5] (It is interesting to observe that each age has found it necessary to produce its own justification for the continuing exclusion of women from ecclesiastical office.) But it would be less than just if I failed to mention that the repre-

---

[5] Typewritten dissertation entitled "Theologische Überlegungen über die Thesis 'Subiectum ordinationis est solus mas' ".

sentatives of this view concede the existence of suprahistorical and valid counterobjections to the whole complex of arguments ranged against the woman in medieval times, just as they willingly admit the type of social or historical barrier that limited Jesus' own choice: he did not select women to be apostles because the social and legal status of women at that time prohibited it. However, other reasons of a more representative type have taken firm root, the favorite being that only a man can represent Christ.[6] Perhaps this is as good a stage as any to recall that in 1 Corinthians 11, 3 there is a clear reference to a woman-Christ parallel.

Most representatives of opponent group B hold an ecclesiastical post of one type or another (catechists, pastoral work, sodalities, social work, etc.). Among this group there is probably no one who would herself wish to be a priest, although many of them hold quite high positions and carry out their duties ably. This is a sign of the times that should not be overlooked. These are women who in fact exercise lay functions and who nowadays are able to find so much scope for action within them as to feel themselves adequately fulfilled. Personally, I take my stand with their viewpoint.[7]

Of those in favor, it can be said of group A that its voices are few and loud even when solidly backed by organized associations such as the St. Joan's Alliance. However much the women in this group maintain that they act the way they do for reasons of personal vocation (the case of a female minister of the Evangelical Church who has turned to Catholicism and is therefore prevented from continuing her vocation is of course a most difficult one), the fact remains that their frequently ill-advised tactics have irritated numerous bishops and so harmed their cause.

Not surprisingly, the theology of their case also leaves much to be desired. Nowadays, one ought to have enough historical

---

[6] J. F. Görres, "Über die Weihe von Frauen zu Priesterinnen", in *Der Christliche Sonntag,* 17 (1965).

[7] Cf. my own comments in the final chapter of *Die Frau und ihr Auftrag* (Freiburg, 1965[2]), pp. 272–81; also *Das Bild der Frau heute* (Dusseldorf, 1967[2]); *Mann und Frau in Familie und Öffentlichkeit* (Munich, 1964); *Die Frau im Aufbruch der Kirche* (Munich, 1964).

sense to realize that indignant complaints levelled at St. Thomas Aquinas and others on account of their apparent blindness to the female cause are quite without logic, for anyone who has completed a course in theology should be aware that, Aquinas' outlook being based upon Aristotelian biology and hylomorphism, he could not have thought otherwise, and in this particular matter is neither a suitable referee nor an authoritative interpreter of the Church's teaching.

And there is certainly no case for turning the question of the woman's admission to ecclesiastical office into a straight demand for compensation in return for having been left out in the cold for so long. "The female sex was suppressed for thousands of years and in this process the Church had, and still has, her share of guilt, in view of the mark her approach to womanhood has left upon the Christian consciousness." [8]

To recapitulate: it is this group's ambition to see women included within the hierarchy, and this goal they entertain without having given any prior thought to reform of ecclesiastical office as such. The group's representatives approach the matter, therefore, as though a basic personal right were at stake.

Free from fanaticism, more flexible and much more sympathetic is group B or those in favor of admitting women to the priesthood (most of this group's representatives are Dutch). Their starting point is that of complementarity in all spheres of human life, and they see no good reason why this complementarity should not also be realized within the Church's ministry. They expect to see this come about as a natural development, not as a reform forced through for its own sake, the removal of the barrier to a reserved profession, or as the realization of ultimate emancipation. "The Church—or at least her hierarchy—is often called a solicitous mother. It is an image that looks a little empty when the motherly care is ultimately exercised only by men." [9]

[8] Cf. Gertrud Heinzelmann, *Wir Schweigen nicht länger* (Zurich, 1964), p. 20 (a pamphlet in German and English).

[9] R. J. A. van Eyden, *loc. cit.,* p. 357.

However illustrative that observation might be, we must ensure that no exaggerated value is placed upon "motherliness", or the woman's special contribution in view of her psychological difference from the male. Care must be taken that progress is not purchased with a return to the traditional image of the woman, for it seems that we become increasingly unable to define the "typically feminine" in any precise fashion. Ultimately we must be prepared to credit a Church willing to discuss openly the reform of ecclesiastical office with the right to consider the complementarity of the sexes when finalizing her conclusions about the need for a sociological transformation of her structures.

Clearly there is a lot here easier said than done, and it is in fact to the jigsaw pieces that lie between that we must look for evidence that it ever could be meaningful to ordain women to the priesthood. Baldly stated, the question is whether or not it is necessary to modern Christianity and the continuing life of the Church, given the present form of the priestly office, to ordain women. If we are honest we must admit that it is not, however conscious we are that Christianity and Church without the co-operation of female members are inconceivable. Perhaps we shall not see women as priests until the office of the president of the eucharistic assembly has changed so radically that its occupant can no longer be called a priest. At that stage we would probably renew the old experience that what mankind is and is not capable of is exemplified with particular clarity in the woman.

Furthermore, the slogan "priest shortage" is not only an outdated term as far as the sociology of religion is concerned (shortages exist in many fields in which roles were once filled by priests) but is also a quite inadequate catchword for furthering the female cause.[10] Let us be quite clear about the fact that a woman is simply not suited to ecclesiastical office as we know it today. Only when it has been transformed from within, and

[10] Anita Röper sees the priest shortage as an issue favoring the ordination of women in "Weibliches Priestertum?" in *Orientierung*, 31 (1967), pp. 93f. She speaks deceptively of female priests as an "emergency solution". This type of argument is as invalid as it would be were one to regard lay activity as an "emergency solution".

reconstituted in relation to the community as a whole, might it become something transferable to women.

With that the discussion might be closed were it not for its recent renewal through the recurrence of the diaconate problem. On the face of it, here, too, the same arguments might be applied: the diaconate for women is at the moment as fruitless a goal as the priesthood. Now that national hierarchies have the option of ordaining lay people to the diaconate, lay people now have (for the first time since primitive Christianity) the opportunity of developing their status to its full potential. By remaining a lay person one increases the potential.

To a certain extent this attitude is a little one-sided. We must realize that seen from the outside Christianity and Church are judged simply as sociological entities, and internal ecclesial debates will have to show an awareness of this. Anyone who lived in a non-Christian country while the Council was in progress will have had plenty of opportunity to hear such judgments. As far as the diaconate is concerned, the exclusion of women would undoubtedly create the impression that the Catholic Church was taking a retrograde step as regards any acceptable attitude to women. And the corollary, of course, is that if it is intended to exclude women even from the diaconate, new possibilities for ecclesial activity are open to men.

What, then, of the diaconate? The unmistakable indignation among the German laity over the reinstitution of this office was supported by Walter Dirks when he pointed out that all necessary ecclesiastical functions not already undertaken by priests can be carried out by lay people and that there is, therefore, no need for a special diaconate, at least not in Germany.[11]

Those in favor of the reinstitution of the diaconate counter this objection with the well-known Catholic rejoinder, "Let us have both": i.e. lay participation and the diaconate. But will the layman still feel up to it when he sees that his new or recently recovered functions are now carried out by ordained deacons? The eventual upshot would surely be a return to a passive, ac-

[11] Cf. *Mann in der Zeit* (Feb., 1967), p. 20.

quiescent laity cared for by an active diaconate and the same old story all over again. It is in this respect more than disappointing to find the following perfidious piece of reasoning in a German diocesan magazine which says that the increased measure of lay involvement "is to be welcomed as a most suitable temporary solution to the diaconate problem", while at the same time declaring its concern that the extension of the lay potential "might be regarded as a method of making the diaconate superfluous".[12]

It is pointless to declare the deacon a sort of hermaphrodite figure consisting of priest and layman (cf. the contradictory appellation "lay-deacon"). The diaconate is precisely a feature of that conception of hierarchy that places value on rank. It is a piece of institutionalization, not to say clericalization, and has little connection with the radical concept of the People of God, the collegiality of the bishops and the mutual support of all types and in all spheres that ecclesiastical office and lay status require from one another in the Church. This is a contradiction, a mixture of irreconcilable notions, that originated with the Council itself.

The only positive aspect of the diaconate discussion lies in the fact that through its rejuvenation we are now one step nearer a married priesthood and a solution of the celibacy question. This is not to say that we should simply do away with celibacy altogether, but merely that it should be made optional, so those who choose it as a way of life will do so freely, regarding it as a charism rather than an imposed obligation. This is an outlook gaining ground among the Dutch clergy and elsewhere. At some future date, then, the Church would have married and unmarried priests, and the diaconate could be the first step in this direction.

No more than that can be said in favor of the diaconate. If one considers that in Germany ecclesiastical functions open to the laity are at present exercised by men and women in the numerical proportion of 1 to 10, and if this relatively small hand-

---

[12] J. Hornef, "Macht eine stärkere Heranziehung des Laien zu diakonischen Functionen den Diakon überflüssig?" in *Pastoralblatt für die Diözesen Aachen, Berlin, Essen, Cologne* (Sept., 1967), p. 273.

ful of men were now to become deacons while the women re-tained their lay status, then the object of reinstituting the diac-onate really does appear highly questionable. The situation is so absurd that one could easily be led to the ironic conclusion that men need a special grace to fulfill functions in the Church which women carry out just as effectively by virtue of being hu-mans and Christians.

We have now seen how, as a direct result of reinstituting the diaconate, the question of women and ecclesiastical office has once more, and in unhappy fashion, become acute. Personally I would beg those concerned to think very carefully before imple-menting the power they now have to ordain deacons. And if it is a step that can no longer be avoided, then even if this means being somewhat unfaithful to my own principles and theological convictions, I would urge that if we are to have deacons at all, let us have both male and female deacons.

Jan Peters, O.C.D./*Smakt-Venray, Netherlands*

Is There Room for Women in the Functions of the Church?

The question of women's place in ecclesiastical functions can be approached from different angles. From the angle of Canon Law one may ask whether this law, as it stands today, leaves room for a woman-priest, and the answer is, briefly and definitely, no. But the theologian cannot leave it at this. He can look for reasons why there is no room for women in the priesthood. He will then find a number of answers which he must admit are influenced by an antiquated image of man, or by a rationalization of ill-understood emotional arguments, or by the use of scriptural texts like "Women should keep silence in church" (1 Cor. 14, 34) that are clearly influenced by contemporary cultural environment. He could also examine the function in itself and find that the theological interpretation is broader today than formerly. Such a broader conception of the function includes the possibility for woman to offer her specific qualities to serve the mediation of salvation. Indeed, salvation is not only mediated through cultural actions (preaching and the administration and celebration of the sacraments) but through one's whole humanity, just as Jesus did not redeem us through one single action (e.g., the death on the cross) but through his whole life, the specific way in which he lived his humanity.

What I hope to do here is to open up anew a question to

which we thought we already had the answer and which therefore seemed no longer an open question.

The subject is topical, perhaps more so in Protestant theology (which has another conception of the ecclesiastical office) than in Catholic theology where the priestly function is one of the classic seven sacraments. To us, with our attitude toward life today, which we all share, the following question would appear quite normal: Is woman, with her own kind of humanity and her own view of religious reality, not capable of making a creative contribution to the Church's positive mission which is to mediate salvation *now,* for people of today? I propose to deal with this under four headings: (1) What do the Old and New Testaments have to say about this? (2) How did woman come to be excluded from ecclesiastical office? (3) Does the emancipation of woman not demand that we reevaluate our position? and (4) How does contemporary theology try to find for woman a place of her own within the scope of sacramental function?

I

THE PLACE OF WOMAN IN THE MEDIATION OF SALVATION

(a) *The Old Testament*

1. *The Negative Aspect:* The Old Testament does not exclude woman from an active role in the mediation of salvation. This mediation takes place in a history of people, men *and* women. No doubt, within this history the image of woman shows restrictions that are similar to those found in the religions and cultures which surrounded Israel, but a close look makes it clear that theological reflection on Genesis, for instance, underlines woman's equality with man. Man is not the complete human being; Adam asks for a helpmate at the human level, and so we read: "Let us make man in our image . . . Male and female he created them" (Gen. 1, 26–7). God sees his likeness realized in his creation of the "human being", not in man or woman in isolation.

God entrusts his creation to both man and woman as equal partners, *in view of salvation.*

2. *The Positive Aspect:* This general view is embodied in various figures of the Old Testament. Salvation in the Old Testament is not an abstract value; it takes shape in tangible realities such as legislation, the expansion of the people, the conquest of a nation, the government of the people, religious renewal. It is interesting that Moses the legislator is accompanied by Aaron's sister Miriam (Ex. 15, 20). The growth of the population is also seen as part of salvation and it belongs to the promise contained in the covenant (Gen. 15, 5) that the number of Abraham's descendants will be like that of the stars in the firmament and like the grains of sand on the seashore. Israel sees therefore the maternal function of woman as a function of salvation. When Israel achieves victories—and this, too, is salvation—it is not only men who are mentioned but also women such as Deborah (Judges 4, and the splendid song of victory in Judges 5, 7: "The peasantry ceased in Israel, they ceased until you arose, Deborah, arose as a mother in Israel"), Judith (16, 7) and Esther. Side by side with the male prophets who inaugurate a religious renewal in Israel, we find also the prophetess Huldah (2 Kgs. 22, 14). Side by side with David the king stands Esther the queen.

It is clear that we cannot limit woman's saving function to a particular office, precisely because salvation is more than cult. One may wonder why woman is never a priest in the Old Testament. But the priestly function in the Old Testament is but one of the functions that mediate salvation, namely, the one concerned with cult. Woman's active role in the mediation of salvation is not denied when one only says that woman cannot be a priest.

Moreover, this might well be a reaction against the pagan priestesses, just as at the beginning there were no official priests in Israel as a reaction against the surrounding nations where the priest was linked with idolatry.

There are also more down-to-earth factors: in actual fact, the priestly function in Israel was a man's work. Quantities of cattle had to be slaughtered for the official sacrifices. During the early period the patriarchal system prevailed where men are the heads of the tribe and fathers the priests of the tribe: a priesthood on a family basis. Nor should one forget that the Levitical priesthood was inherited and in this way reserved to the descendants of Aaron.

In general, the Old Testament gives sufficient evidence that woman had indeed an active part to play in the mediation of salvation.

(b) *The New Testament*

Before passing on to an assessment of the data of the New Testament, I would like to point out that the concrete and tangible reality that shaped the form of salvation in the Old Testament became obscure in the days of Jesus. The monarchy had disappeared; there was no peace; there was no victory; the law provided no more inspiration and was "dead". Yet, there was a Messianism, but the content of this expectation of salvation was so indefinite and subject to such varied interpretations that Jesus refused to identify himself with any of the traditional concrete expressions of salvation in the Old Testament: monarchy, law, prophecy. Moreover, Jesus is in fact the new and fuller concrete expression of salvation. He is the way, the truth, the life, the manna, the law, the king and the prophet. In short, he is the full embodiment of salvation. Salvation is no longer a concrete situation but a concrete person: this Jesus. In this way salvation is personified, deepened and spiritualized.

The question of woman's active role in the mediation of salvation now becomes the concrete question about the active role of woman in relation to this historical Jesus and further, in relation to the Christ of faith.

Insofar as woman's active role in relation to this Jesus is concerned we now find suddenly a rich source of information in Luke the evangelist. The religious interpretation of woman as mother in the Old Testament finds its fulfillment in the unexpected perspective of Jesus' childhood narrative. Here God "has regarded the low estate of his handmaiden" (Lk. 1, 48). "And behold, you will conceive in your womb and bear a son, and you shall call his name Jesus" (God saves). Then follow the concrete expressions of salvation: "He will be great, and will be called the Son of the Most High; and the Lord God will give to him the throne of his father David, and he will reign over the house of Jacob forever; and of his kingdom there will be no end" (Lk. 1, 31–4). Women are actively involved in Jesus' public life and are witnesses of his resurrection. For Jesus himself the sexual distinction between man and woman is particularly unimportant, a fact which astonishes even his disciples (cf. Jn. 4, 27). There is no need to develop here the first part of the question any further. There remains, however, the far more difficult question: What is woman's active role in relation to the Christ of faith? Everyone will agree with the general observation that salvation will henceforth consist in perpetuating this Christ in whom all divisions cease: "There is neither Jew nor Greek, there is neither slave nor free, there is neither male nor female" (Gal. 3, 28). When we listen without prejudice to the writings of the New Testament, we shall realize that this process of continuation is no longer concerned with men *or* women, but with men *and* women, "people" or "human persons". The biological contrasts have been overcome in principle.

In the writings of the New Testament we meet with the names of women who, alone or with their husbands and families, give themselves to the service of the "saints". Recently converted women occupy a central position in the community. Women risk their lives, are persecuted. Why? Because they know to whom they bear witness.

In Acts 1, 14 we see women persevering in prayer together with Mary the mother of Jesus. Without any sexual discrimination women are mentioned here with the apostles and the brothers of Jesus. Women share in the approval of the choice of Matthias who must take Judas' place in the apostolic college.

In Acts 2, 16–8, where Peter uses Joel's prophecy in order to explain what really happened at the first Pentecost, woman,

on whom the Spirit has also been poured out, is far from being
the inferior and inarticulate creature that must be veiled and
kept silent in the community: "Yea, and on my manservants
and my maidservants in those days I shall pour out my Spirit,
and they shall prophesy." Where the Spirit of God is clearly
poured out without measure it would be arrogant to limit his
action to one sex. When we do that, we shall probably "quench
the Spirit", at least partially (1 Thess. 5, 19).

Acts 21, 9 shows indeed that the four daughters of Philip the
evangelist did in fact possess this gift of prophecy. The care of
the poor (Acts 9, 36f.) is a service not restricted to men only
but is exercised to the full by Tabitha, a disciple in the town of
Joppa. As teacher it is Priscilla who takes part in explaining
God's way to the eloquent Apollos of Alexandria (Acts 18, 26).
It is therefore more than a polite formula when Paul calls her
and her husband his collaborators. I am well aware of the fact
that the "office", in the loaded meaning we give today to that
word, is but vaguely described in the writings of the New Testament. We may nevertheless conclude that the active mediation
and continuation of the Christ of faith, our salvation, is not
limited to man and that woman plays a full part in this process.

How, then, did later theology come to have such a limited
conception of the office that woman was positively excluded
from it?

II

THE HISTORICAL RESTRICTION OF THE PRIESTLY OFFICE AND THE EXCLUSION OF WOMAN FROM THIS SPECIFIC FUNCTION

During the first three centuries of the young Christian movement we constantly see women exercise functions which today
we would call priestly functions. We see them administer baptism, give the eucharist to the sick and the children; she is
ordained, has a place in the hierarchy and belongs to the clergy.
This situation begins to change when Christianity turns from

being a movement to being an institution. In 313 Christianity became an established religion under Constantine. The functional apparatus of the Roman State begins to be taken over by the Church. There is also a considerable difference between Eastern and Western Christianity.

In assisting the apostle, woman deployed a rich activity in the East, and mainly on three lines: as Christian prophetess (principally in Montanist and Gnostic circles), in catechetical and missionary work and as deaconesses. Here woman became indispensable, even for the imposition of hands on the sick. The function of the widow as deaconess was exercised autonomously in various ways. We even see women put on the same level with the presbyters. This situation was widespread in Syria, Egypt and in Byzantium which later on detached itself from a centralizing Rome. But this expansion did not happen without struggle. Insofar as rank is concerned the East placed her between the higher and the lower clergy. She bound herself to lifelong service after the imposition of hands and the reception of the stole from the bishop. In the West, too, a ritual remained in force which was applied to women and resembled the ordination to the priesthood. Later on it passed into the consecration of an abbess or a canoness.

In the West the gradual exclusion of woman concentrated principally on functions that were typically presbyteral and liturgical. Where the function is narrowed down to the offering of the sacrifice, woman is explicitly excluded from the service of the altar.

In the Middle Ages the image of woman must be seen against a threefold background:

1. the anti-feminism, prevailing in the Church and in theology;

2. the erotic culture of the troubadour who limited the dignity of woman to partnership in love;

3. the beginnings of civilian emancipation in religion and politics. During the Middle Ages woman was mainly valued as possession and as labor force. The consecration of a woman as abbess with jurisdiction persists even in the Middle Ages.

To this we must add that the 12th century saw the beginning of the definition of the sacrament as a sign that signifies and gives grace while ecclesial office was seen as the sacrament of orders and included among the seven sacraments. This encouraged the conviction that only man can be the sign of Jesus as the sole Priest. But during this same period there were still deaconesses in Constantinople and therefore in the Eastern Church.

Woman was left with being mother or virgin, while virginity became religiously overrated. Historically, then, man became the bearer of the restricted priesthood. It is this factual situation, the fruit of a cultural and historical development, which became the object of theological study and led to the assertion that only a baptized man can be the bearer of a Christian office. I shall come back to this kind of symbolic reasoning in my fourth point.

It is rather curious that the Reformation, which pretended to return to the Christian origins, brought no correction on this point. In their view of woman in the Church the reformers in general followed the prevailing opinion and accepted her position as willed by God. Reasons for this exclusion of woman were found in 1 Corinthians 14, 34f. and 1 Timothy 2, 11, and this was thought conclusive. 1 Corinthians 14, 34 reads: "As in all the churches of the saints, the women should keep silence in the churches. For they are not permitted to speak, but should be subordinate, as even the law says." And 1 Timothy 2, 11: "Let a woman learn in silence with all submissiveness."

In Luther there is no exclusion of woman from preaching in principle. In matters of office the reformers emphasized the service of the Word. Although Luther maintained at first (1516) that leadership in worship and preaching was reserved to man because woman was much more liable to superstition and occultism, he said in 1522: "If it happens that no man is present a woman can take charge and preach before others as far as she is able." Woman is no longer excluded, and this on the ground of such biblical data as the universal priesthood of the faithful, but man is still thought to be more suited. Calvin wants both more and less than that. He wants more in contrast with Luther who left the care of the poor to the State: he wanted a genuine care of the poor and the sick in the Church, although this was not incorporated in his Church Order. He wanted less in that he forbade woman to baptize, speak and teach in the Church. She can have no public function apart from the diaconate.

III

WHAT PLACE OF HER OWN CAN MODERN THEOLOGY FIND FOR WOMAN WITHIN THE SCOPE OF THE SACRAMENTAL OFFICE?

What has been said so far can be summarized as follows:

1. Exegetically there is no compelling argument for the exclusion of woman from office.

2. The actual exclusion of woman from office can be sufficiently shown to be an historical development to deprive it of any absolute claims or any assumption that it is "obvious".

3. The Christian concept of office as a charismatic mediation and service instead of a juridical concept compels the Catholic theologian, too, to investigate the specific place and contribution of woman within the priestly office and to ask himself whether woman cannot have a mediating function in a broader and more scriptural view of the office.

After the inevitable declericalization of the office[1] broader and higher demands will be made upon the office-bearer than in the time when the sacred still formed a world apart, with definite and clear boundaries. In those days one could still "learn" how to be a priest: to say Mass, to preach, to baptize, etc. Today the situation is that man must be helped in a reality that has lost its clear contours and from within which he has to look for the meaning of his existence. The office-bearer must show him the way, help him to find it with the aid of the Gospel. He must help his fellow-Christian in giving a meaning to existence. All this demands of the office-bearer a *greater competence,* not only *intellectually,*

[1] Cf. Ivan Illich, "Métamorphose du Clergé," in *Esprit,* 364 (Oct. 1967), pp. 584–601.

but also in *religious ability*. This religious element is a special dimension in human existence, just as the ethical element and the esthetic. Some people are more religiously gifted, others less. This religious giftedness, a psychical structure, is a natural ability which is not equally possessed by all. This psychical structure is confirmed and underlined in the ordination; it is not created then, it is not a *creatio ex nihilo*.

The office-bearer will discover that his competence is mostly required for the sharing in, and interpretation of, the basic questions of existence in their religious dimension. This religious dimension is precisely the essential element of both Christianity and the leader. This leader does not walk ahead in isolation but has people round him. It is true that it is difficult here to say exactly what is, and what is not, sacramental. Take, for instance, confession and penitential services. Who can say here where the boundary of the function runs? There will have to be definite key points around which the functions are set out. Starting with Christ, who opened the new world to mankind, we shall have to find out what exactly our mission is.

The office must be shaped anew constantly by men themselves. In every age it must have a face that is recognizable and can be turned to. But this implies that the office must be human as far as possible, must show as many human aspects, variations, gifts and adaptations as possible.

For this reason one ought to admit that woman has a place in this office. Does the Church not damage her own image when she thinks that all her features must be male features? This is rather an impoverishment. Modern anthropology has made it only too clear that "human" means male *and* female. Man and woman together must fashion and exercise the office so that each can exercise it in a less one-sided manner. The *human* exercise of office demands an extension of the office so that it can be borne by both man and woman.

Does this give woman a place in the Church's office (I deliberately avoid the term "priest")? The only argument that holds water is the sociological one. The position of woman in the

Church's office depends on her position in a given culture. The question is whether woman is accepted and whether she can fulfill a function usefully and efficiently. When we see how the office developed from the New Testament throughout history we find that the direction of this development has been for a large part determined by the Church herself. We may therefore ask whether in our own age, too, the Church is not competent to create new forms of office for women. There would be no harm in the Church as mother being productive for once. When we look at the office in the New Testament there does not seem to be much that was meant to be everlasting. On the other hand, we *do* see in both the Old and the New Testaments that God means specific people to be appointed to the office of mediation. Christ himself is chosen and chooses others in turn. This persisting element of a choice by God is essential to the office in the Bible.

Our approach should therefore be in the following direction. For us salvation is not a *thing* but a human value: the salvation of concrete persons. This salvation, which has assumed a personal form in Christ, must be mediated by the Church, and she does this through her office. This office, then, already embraces more human elements than merely the service of Word and sacraments. We should therefore start by looking at salvation in a broader perspective than that of a separate sphere of human reality or something that is added from outside to man as an existing entity. Only when we see this shall we also see that this extended office cannot be borne only by the male. This would damage the content of salvation. Nor should it be borne only by the female of the species. It is an office commissioned to human beings and sexual discrimination should be eliminated. This will become obvious when the office is more humanized. Modern anthropology has pointed out that there are no such things as exclusively male or female qualities. We have to try, on the basis of a distinct biological distinction, to be human, Christian and capable of bearing office, and thus to mediate salvation.

Are we not beginning to realize that to determine the Gospel as doctrine, as a rational and well thought-out dogma, is necessary but not everything? Should the manipulation of an instrument of power such as excommunication not be entrusted to women as well as men? The first question of an office-bearer should not be whether he is a man or whether office can also be bestowed on a woman, but how humanity can, as completely as possible, be put to the service of mediating salvation.

All the literature dealing at present with this problem still shows a vast difference in mentality. It is quite possible that if the Council had attempted to pronounce on it, the result would have been negative because the majority of the fathers had not yet reached this stage. Humanity is only complete in man and woman together, and on the basis of this argument I would suggest that the admission of women to ecclesiastical office is not only possible but desirable. It seems to me that this way of looking at the problem has overcome the kind of symbolic reasoning which has for so long dominated the discussion of "the ordination of women". Our modern sensitivity to symbols can no longer conclude that since Scripture presents God as male and since the historical Jesus was a man, the mediator of God's salvation in the Church of Christ must also be a man.

We must also dare to accept the theological conclusion that a truly "catholic", i.e., universal, office is incompatible with a practice based on biological and cultural differentiation. This should clearly not lead to woman merely imitating man's office as practiced up till now in the Western Church.[2] The monopoly of a clericalized office seems to be a thing of the past, and with

[2] For a good bibliographical survey see *Kosmos en Oecumene*, 2 (1967). The World Union of Women's Organizations has incorporated this topic in its congress to take place in Rome, 1968. Just as the World Council of Churches has a special department for "Woman in the Order of the Church", the Willibrordsvereniging (Society of St. Willibrord) of Holland is planning a special secretariate for this question. One of the resolutions passed by the Third World Congress for the Lay Apostolate ran as follows: "The Third World Congress for the Lay Apostolate wishes to express its desire that women be granted by the Church full rights and responsibilities as Christians, and a serious doctrinal study be undertaken into the place of women within the sacramental order and within the Church" (*The Tablet*, October 28, 1967), p. 1138.

it the security mechanisms with which man used to defend his office against the intrusion of woman. My plea for a place for woman in office is not a plea for imitation or copying but for the full humanity of the office and the oneness in Christ, on the lines of St. Paul: "There is neither Jew nor Greek, there is neither slave nor free; there is neither male nor female, for you are all one in Christ Jesus" (Gal. 3, 28). This does away in principle with all discrimination of race, class or sex.

PART II
BIBLIOGRAPHICAL
SURVEY

Henry Chadwick/*Oxford, England*

The Discussion about Anglican
Orders in Modern Anglican Theology

The quest for a via media—the Anglican ideal observable since the first moments of its emergence as a distinct type of Church pattern—is nowhere more apparent than in the Anglican doctrine of holy orders. If it has been insufficiently "sacerdotal" to satisfy Roman Catholic feelings, it has been altogether too traditional and catholicizing to be acceptable to left-wing Protestants holding Zwinglian or Puritan positions. And yet it has constituted at least a conscientious attempt to preserve a duly proportioned, balanced and apostolic faith, grounded on Holy Scripture and deeply respectful toward the tradition of the Christian society. It is not too much to say that the long-standing controversy concerning English orders is an epitome of the entire debate about the Anglican understanding of the Church and sacraments. Inevitably, therefore, in a period of lively ecumenical conversation among separated brethren, the problem can never move far from the center of the stage.

The controversy about Anglican orders has a long and extremely complicated history. But its basic, elemental terms of reference are simple enough. Sometimes their permanence seems all too intractable and indestructible. For the attempt to contain, in a positive sense, both Catholic and Protestant affirmations about the ministry is built into the foundation document itself, the English Ordinal. The defense of this can be discerned in one

141

of the earliest of all attempts to formulate an Anglican position, namely, in the Thirty-Nine Articles, approved by the Convocation of Canterbury under Archbishop Parker in 1563 in a form very close to their final shape of 1571. The Articles of 1563 were a drastic revision of the much more Protestant Articles of 1553, notably in eliminating a Zwinglian doctrine of the eucharist. Article 36 rebuts two opposing and antithetical criticisms of the English Ordinal of 1550. It affirms that the Ordinal contains all things necessary, and denies that it has anything superstitious. In plain words, the Article is replying to criticisms that the English ordination rites are either so widely divergent from the Latin Pontifical as to lack essential elements or so closely dependent upon it as to be utterly unreformed.

Continually during the last four centuries Anglican theologians can be seen trying to state their doctrine of orders in this controversial, vulnerable situation, open to attack on two fronts simultaneously. It has been axiomatic for Anglican theologians that ordination is a lifelong commission from God, which is mediated not only through an inward sense of vocation and capacity, and not only through the call of the community, but also through the outward act of the laying on of hands with prayer to which an inward gift is attached. The order of the episcopate in due succession is accepted as a sign and instrument of unity and continuity in the Church, by which apostolic oversight of the People of God is exercised. Yet while Anglicans have preserved the rule of episcopal ordination as necessary for their own discipline and Church order, they have usually been reluctant to pass a negative judgment on the ecclesial status of bodies that have lacked episcopal succession. The order of priesthood, unlike the episcopate, has no authority to confirm or to ordain; but the priest is empowered to absolve and to celebrate the eucharist as essential constituents in his total pastoral responsibility for his flock.

The English Ordinal

The Ordinal first appeared in 1550; it was slightly revised in 1552 and 1662. Its authors are not known, but the hand of Archbishop Cranmer may safely be assumed. It provides three distinct services for deacons, priests and bishops, and explains its intention in a Preface to the effect that from the apostles' time the Church has had these three orders, which none may take on himself, but may receive only after due scrutiny and ordination "by prayer with imposition of hands". These traditional orders are to be "continued and reverently . . . esteemed". Accordingly, those already ordained (under the Latin Pontifical) are on no account to be reordained.

The principal controversies have turned upon the "Form of Ordering Priests". Here the liturgical Gospel is separated from the laying on of hands by a solemn charge and interrogatory (derived from a draft by Bucer) concerning the priest's high responsibilities for the souls entrusted to him; by the *Veni Creator*; and by a prayer of thanksgiving for the gift of apostolic ministry and petition for the grace of office. The act of ordination (for which Bucer's draft was significantly rejected) follows at once. There is no anointing of the hands. The bishop, with the priests present, lays hands on each candidate and says: "Receive the Holy Ghost [for the office and work of a priest in the Church of God, now committed unto thee by the imposition of our hands]. Whose sins thou dost forgive, they are forgiven; and whose sins thou dost retain, they are retained. And be thou a faithful dispenser of the Word of God and of his holy sacraments; in the name of the Father, and of the Son, and of the Holy Ghost. Amen." (The bracketed words were added in 1662 because of controversy with Presbyterians.) The *porrectio instrumentorum* follows: in 1550 the Bible was given with the chalice and paten; since 1552 it has been the Bible alone. The accompanying formula runs: "Take thou authority to preach the Word of God and to minister the holy sacraments in the congregation . . ."

This Ordinal quickly attracted sharp criticism from both sides in the 16th century. The Puritans were horrified by the retention of "Receive the Holy Ghost", and regarded it as no better than the Pontifical. Roman Catholics were slower to formulate their objections. They did not like the form or intention, but generally found it easier to try to throw doubt on the preservation of due succession in the consecration of Matthew Parker in 1559 or of his principal consecrator William Barlow. There is no need today to discuss the resultant crop of now discredited legends. In fact the crux of the divergence from the Latin Pontifical clearly lies in the silence of the English Ordinal concerning the priest's power to "offer sacrifice to God and to celebrate Mass both for the living and for the dead". The problem lay in the correct doctrine of eucharistic sacrifice.

The English Ordinal keeps silence at this point. Admittedly the power to offer could easily be held to be implicitly included in the general commission to dispense the holy sacraments. Whatever is done in the eucharist, that the priest is truly empowered to do. But whereas the power of the keys is as explicit as anyone could reasonably desire, nothing is said or necessarily implied about power to offer sacrifice for the living and the dead. The Articles of 1563 speak severely of the "sacrifices of Masses in which . . . the priest did offer Christ for the sick and the dead". They also criticize the doctrine of transubstantiation. It should be remarked that the reasons given are directed exclusively against a crudely physical conception of Christ's presence in the sacred elements, not against the belief (which is strongly affirmed) that after a spiritual manner "the body of Christ is given, taken, and received in the supper". Anglican theology has felt bound to repudiate any implication that anything we can do in the Mass can add to the redeeming work of Christ, but at least since 1600 has been ready to affirm that the eucharist is a representation of the sacrifice of Christ—"Therefore we may be said to offer Christ in a mystery, and to sacrifice him by way of commemoration" (Francis Mason, 1613).

Recent Anglican-Methodist Discussion

In modern Anglican theology the discussion of the doctrine of holy orders continues to revolve round the same, perennial problems of the true meaning of priesthood and sacrifice. Since 1963 this question has become especially sharp in England as a consequence of proposals, put forward by a committee of authorized representatives, for a reconciliation of the English Methodists with the Church of England. In this discussion the fundamental issue has not been the necessity for preserving episcopal succession or even the invariability of episcopal ordination, but rather the precise nature of priesthood. The Committee was given an extremely difficult task to perform. Its first report (1963) was received with mingled gratitude and criticism, and it has now produced a second interim report entitled *Towards Reconciliation* (1967) in which it attempts to meet some of the criticisms. The new report submits a draft Ordinal, but the crux lies in a proposed service of reconciliation by prayer and laying on of hands. According to the scheme, the Anglican bishop is to lay hands on Methodist ministers with prayer for the gift of the Spirit "to endue each, according to his need, with grace for the office and work of a priest", and with a formal commission: "Take authority for the office and work of a priest, to preach the Word of God and to minister the holy sacraments among us as need shall arise and you shall be licensed to do." Then the Anglican clergy are similarly received by the presiding Methodist minister with prayer and laying on of hands. The painful difficulty is evident: Is the bishop ordaining the Methodist ministers or not?

No Methodist has expressed doubt or hesitations about the validity of Anglican orders. The Church of England is not disposed to deny truly ecclesial status to non-episcopal Churches; and no Anglican would be likely even to hesitate about acknowledging the spiritual power and reality of the prophetic ministry found among the Methodists. Nevertheless, since a substantial body of Anglicans are uncertain whether the Methodists lack due authority and juridical validity, the proposed act of reconciliation is so formulated that its form may be sufficient for an ordination if that is required by God. That is to say, however, that the meaning of the act of reconciliation for the Methodist ministers will not be the same for everyone concerned. To many Anglicans the proposed service would undoubtedly be regarded as a conditional or even unconditional ordination of Methodist ministers to a priesthood not hitherto exercised. To others (both Methodist and Anglican) the act could not possibly be interpreted as conferring *presbyterium* without becoming a reordination. Everyone agrees that the repetition of the sacrament would be intolerable.

Because of these difficulties the Committee's proposals have been candidly criticized with some force, and no practical move has yet been made. A crucial point is without doubt the juridical status associated with episcopal ordination. This is sufficiently illustrated by the fact that under English law the service of reconciliation would be regarded as having the legal effect of conferring ordination to the priesthood on Methodist ministers, whatever the private intention of those taking part in it. After attending to further criticism and discussion, the Committee is hoping to produce a final report in 1968. Meanwhile the discussion has stimulated valuable thinking and courteous debate about the nature and function of priesthood.

Roman Catholic and Anglican Discussion

In conclusion, the further question must honestly and candidly be raised whether anything fresh may yet be hoped for from an examination of the papal decision of 1896 regarding the invalidity of Anglican orders. The absolute and unqualified condemnation in the Bull *Apostolicae Curae* has certainly seemed to leave no room for any real maneuver, and for a long time the argument has looked like a complete stalemate. In 1896–98 the utterances on both sides were felt to be painful, and in the contemporary ecumenical dialogue there is still some legacy of embarrassment in dealing with such questions. Nothing said here should be taken to imply or to hint that the time may soon be ripe for an official reconsideration of the problem. But it is evident to all that the possibility of such a reconsideration might become less unreal, and the prospect less gloomy, if some new elements were to be brought into the discussion. That must depend in a substantial degree upon the further researches of

Church historians, and upon the reflections of theologians concerning the basic principles of sacramental theology in general and the requisite form and intention in particular.

Historians of today can tell us more than their predecessors in 1896 both about ancient forms of ordination and about the history of the English Reformation. Indeed (I think it will be generally conceded), both in the papal Bull and in the *Answer* of the English archbishops, some of the historical assertions can only be described as rash, misleading and plainly wrong. Of the old, jangling arguments and counterarguments whether Parker and Barlow were duly consecrated the Bull of 1896 happily said not a word. Historians now think it sure that the succession was preserved. The ghost of the old argument concerning the *porrectio instrumentorum* has ceased to haunt the streets, and was already dismissed as irrelevant in the Bull. The central problem remains the theological question of form and intention.

The criticism that the Anglican form is defective, formulated in the Bull of 1896, is one that Anglican theologians and historians have had the greatest difficulty in understanding, not only on their own presuppositions but even on Roman Catholic assumptions. According to *Apostolicae Curae* the English "Form of Ordering Priests" is insufficient because, between 1550 and 1662, the words used at the actual conferment of priest's orders did not specifically mention what order was being conferred. (In 1662 the controversy with the Presbyterians led to revision, and since 1662 the order of priesthood has been explicitly named at this point.) Nevertheless, the old form had no ambiguity about it. The service prescribed mentions priesthood so many times that the meaning and purpose of the rite in this respect could not conceivably be regarded as doubtful. Only someone who slept throughout the service, waking up only during the two seconds during which the bishop said "Receive the Holy Ghost", could possibly have experienced any hesitation about the precise order that was being conferred.

The question of intention, however, is more complicated, and it is at this point that the discussion has become intricate.

Anglican theology has not been willing to grant that the commission given in ordination remains unaffected if the ordained minister, whether deacon, priest or bishop, becomes separated from the body of the Church. On this ground the Anglican Church has never accepted the validity of ordinations bestowed by *episcopi vagantes*. In keeping with this general attitude, the doctrine of intention most widely current among Anglicans has been external rather than internal. Probably in consequence of this prevalent attitude, most Anglican theologians (until very recently) seem to have assumed that when *Apostolicae Curae* criticized the English Ordinal for its defect of intention the Bull was denying the external corporate intention of the Anglican Church to do what the Church does. Father Clark (*Anglican Orders and Defect of Intention,* London, 1956) has argued that, of the many possible interpretations of *Apostolicae Curae,* this at least can hardly be what the Bull meant. He proposed to interpret the Bull to mean that a positive intention to exclude the conferment of a sacrificing priesthood nullifies the general (admitted) Anglican intention to do what the Church does. If this presupposes that users of the English Ordinal had in 1559, and indeed still now have, a deliberate will to reject orthodox eucharistic doctrine, Anglican theologians are likely to remain very mystified.

One last point deserves mention, albeit with the greatest diffidence. In 1896 (as readers of his biography will well know) Cardinal Vaughan, Archbishop of Westminster, strongly believed that the reunion of the Church of England with the Holy See could come about exclusively by the submission of individual Anglicans to the Roman obedience, not by any "corporate reunion". It was confidently expected that a papal declaration of the complete invalidity of Anglican orders would quickly produce a landslide of converts among High Anglican clergy. It was deeply feared that a recognition of validity or even of doubtful validity (with consequent ordination *sub conditione*) would merely have the result of confirming the old Anglican spirit of independence from Roman authority. To the historian of today, looking back on the principal documents and the chief actors in the drama (Lord Halifax, T. A. Lacey, Aidan Gasquet, and Moyes), it is sadly evident that the consequences for both participating groups were different from what they had attempted to achieve. Moreover, the manner in which the discussion was conducted left a hard legacy of ill-feeling and distrust. The question of the validity or invalidity of Anglican orders is evidently one of truth, to be settled without regard to the consequences. Nevertheless, a consideration of the possible consequences may at least predispose the will. As long as there remain those (whether Roman Catholic or Anglican) who hope and pray for an eventual reunion between Rome and Canterbury, there will always be some who want to discover some way of deliverance from imprisonment in the legacy of the past. Perhaps Cardinal Vaughan's position will remain in force, and corporate reunion is a dangerous dream. But if it ever comes to be felt that he might have been wrong, or that his position was right in the 19th century but ought not to become a fixed stance for all time, then perhaps it may become possible to explain *Apostolicae Curae* in such a way that it does not bring all conversation to an abrupt stop.

BIBLIOGRAPHY

The controversy of 1896–8 produced three basic documents: the Bull *Apostolicae Curae*, the *Answer of the English Archbishops* (by John Wordsworth and Mandell Creighton), and Cardinal Vaughan's rejoinder, *A Vindication of the Bull "Apostolicae Curae"*. For later Anglican comment see T. A. Lacey, *A Roman Diary* (London, 1910); R. C. Moberly, *Ministerial Priesthood* (London, 1897); an Orthodox assessment in A. Bulgakoff, *The Question of Anglican Orders* (London, 1899). The best short statement by a modern Anglican remains Gregory Dix, O.S.B., *The Question of Anglican Orders* (London, 1956). Cf. John J. Hughes, "Recent Studies of the Validity of Anglican Orders," in *Concilium* 31, pp. 135–46. For an Anglican comment on Fr. Clark's study see E. L. Mascall, "Intention and Form in Anglican Orders," in *Church Quarterly Review* 158 no. 326 (1957), pp. 4–20. The literature provoked by Anglican/Methodist debates consists of short pamphlets; nothing is as important as the actual reports of the Commission concerned.

Hilaire Marot, O.S.B. / *Chevetogne, France*

The Orthodox Churches and Anglican Orders

From September 1–15, 1966, an inter-Orthodox commission held meetings in Belgrade. It prepared the topics which the Third Rhodes Conference (November, 1964) had put on the agenda for discussions between the Orthodox Churches and the Anglican Churches. The validity of Anglican orders had to figure prominently in such a dialogue.

The Belgrade meeting provided us with a glimpse into the present-day position of the Orthodox Churches on this delicate and subtle question in Orthodox theology. Obviously, we cannot treat the subject in detail in these few pages. In broad outline, the Orthodox approach is this. The ritual of the Anglican Ordinal is judged to be satisfactory, but "recognition of validity" presupposes a faith that is close to the Orthodox faith or identical with it. This recognition would be granted, either in the case of individual or group conversions of Anglican clergy to Orthodoxy (the Greek position), or with respect to the Anglican hierarchy as such (the Russian tendency); it is not always easy to distinguish between the two. Moreover, this recognition by the Orthodox Churches is often granted by virtue of the "economy".[1]

---

[1] The "economy" is a mitigation of the rigorousness (*akribeia*) of the law, in view of a greater good. The Orthodox Church is regarded as the sole "depository of grace".

I

EARLIEST DECISIONS OF THE AUTOCEPHALOUS CHURCHES

Since they have been brought up in recent days, it would be well to recall earlier decisions made by certain Orthodox Churches. In 1922 the Ecumenical Patriarch (Constantinople) Meletios IV took the initiative of recognizing, along with his Synod, the validity of Anglican orders "on the same level as that of Roman Catholics, Old Catholics and Armenians". He pointed out that this "was not to be regarded as a decision of the whole Orthodox Church, since that would presume that all the other Orthodox Churches were of the same opinion as the Church of Constantinople".

In 1923 the patriarch Damien made an analogous declaration in the name of the Church of Jerusalem. That same year Archbishop Cyril did the same thing in the name of the Cypriot Church. Archbishop Cyril pointed out something that had remained implicit in the other statements. He said he was talking about the case of Anglican clerics who would enter the Orthodox Church without being reordained.

After the Lambeth Conferences of 1930, Patriarch Meletios, now transferred to Alexandria, declared that he was adopting the 1922 decision of Constantinople; he specifically stated that Anglican priests who embraced Orthodoxy would not be reordained.

II

THE BUCHAREST MEETINGS: 1935

A mixed doctrinal commission was convened in October 1931. Represented on it were the four patriarchates of the Near East, Cyprus, Greece and the three Churches of the Balkans; the Russian Church was not represented. This commission was not able to satisfy everyone—the Romanian Church, for example. Despite this, at a meeting in Bucharest from June 1 to June 8,

1935, an Anglican delegation and a commission of the Holy
Synod reached agreement on tradition, apostolic succession, orders, the eucharist, the sacraments and justification.[2]

On March 20, 1936, the Holy Synod recognized the validity
of Anglican Orders (*in se,* it would seem) under one condition:
"The resolution is to become definitive as soon as the supreme
authority of the Anglican Church ratifies all the declarations of
its delegation". After discussion, the Canterbury Convocation
accepted the Bucharest agreement on January 20, 1937; it acknowledged it "to be in accord with the Anglican formularies
and to be a legitimate interpretation of the faith as it has been
handed down in the Church of England".[3] Clearly, there were
certain nuances in this statement.

Adopting the conclusions reached by professors on the faculty
at Athens (Professors Alivisatos, Bratsiotis, Balanos and Trembelas[4]), the Greek Synod was more reserved. On September 21,
1939, it declared that the question fell within the competence
of the entire Orthodox Church and that, in the meantime, the
Greek Church would judge each case of Anglican conversion on
its own merits.

III

CAUTIOUS OVERTURES AT MOSCOW: 1948

After World War II, the Russian Church came to the forefront
at a meeting of the autocephalous Orthodox Churches in Moscow

---

[2] On the Bucharest accords: G. K. A. Bell, *Documents on Christian
Unity* (London, 1948), III, pp. 43–50.

[3] *Chronicle of Convocation,* 1937, 5–24; 71–89.

[4] On these statements within the framework of Greek theology, see:
P. Dumont, "La Chiesa greca et la validità delle ordinazioni anglicane," in
Oriente cristiano (1967). Alivisatos regarded the Anglican doctrine as
being "very orthodox" and in accord with Bucharest; but, in accordance
with Greek theology, he would not go beyond the obligation of not re-
ordaining in the event of a conversion to Orthodoxy. Bratsiotis stressed
the doctrinal variations in Anglicanism and its hesitations after Bucharest.

from July 8–18, 1948. The Bulgarian Metropolitan, Nicodemus of Sliven, was very favorable to overtures, as were the Romanian delegates, Bishop Anthime (see below), and Professor Vintilescu; they were perplexed that the conditions laid down at Bucharest in 1935 had not yet been fully satisfied, but they did not attach too much importance to this.[5]

The Conference as a whole, however, adopted the Russian point of view. They stressed the Protestant aspects but admitted the possibility of recognizing the Anglican hierarchy if certain conditions were fulfilled. The unity of faith and confession would first have to be established between the two groups of Churches; it would have to be formulated in a document that would be authoritative for the Anglican community. All this would be achieved by virtue of the principle of "economy" through a Council of the whole Orthodox Church.[6]

IV

RHODES III AND THE DIALOGUE

Prof. Voronov

In preparation for the opening of a general dialogue between the Orthodox and the Anglicans, Liverij Voronov (of Leningrad) published a study in 1964. It was not without merit, but it was based in large part on the works of Russian theologians prior to the Revolution. Having examined the "credal books" (39 Articles and *Prayer Book*), he briefly considered those Anglo-Catholic interpretations which "offer little hope of rapprochement". But

[5] *Proceedings of the Conference of Autocephalous Churches* (Moscow, 1948), I, pp. 292–312, 315–32.

[6] *Ibid.*, II, pp. 445–47. Apropos of the tendency of Russian theology, see Metropolitan Serge, "The Attitude of Christ's Church towards the Communities Separated from Her," in *Zhurnal Moskovskoy Patriarchii* (1931,–2,–3,–4); *One Church*, 1955, n. 1, 2. *Idem*, "The Meaning of Apostolic Succession in Heterodoxy," in *Zhurnal Moskovskoy Patriarchii* (1935); reproduced *ibid.*, 1961, 10, pp. 30–45, and *Messager de l'exarchat*, 42/43 (1963), pp. 74–96.

he concluded that they were not precise enough to reach any final decision on them.[7]

Romanians and Anglicans

After it had been decided to initiate a full dialogue between the Orthodox and Anglican Churches (Rhodes, November 1964), Dr. Ramsey visited Patriarch Justinian of Romania the following year (June 2–8, 1965). It was precisely thirty years after the Bucharest meetings of the 1930's. "I have no doubt," said Dr. Ramsey, "that future conferences will confirm those accords and will lead to further agreements."

From June 21–28, 1966, Patriarch Justinian visited London, accompanied by Bishop Anthime. The Patriarch "reminded the Archbishop that, on the preceding June 6, the Holy Synod of Romania had fully adopted the agreements reached by the two Churches after the Bucharest Conference of 1935". Both sides hoped that "relations between the Orthodox Church and the Churches of the Anglican Communion might be able to make further progress on the basis of those prior agreements".[8]

V

TWO TENDENCIES AT BELGRADE: SEPTEMBER 1966

An inter-Orthodox commission was set up to prepare the agenda for the dialogue at Belgrade.[9] Within this commission

[7] L. Voronov, "The Question of the Anglican Hierarchy in the Light of Orthodox Theology," in *Travaux théologiques*, 3 (Moscow, 1964), pp. 64–144 (in Russian); *Messager de l'exarchat*, 54–55 (1966), pp. 75–112; 56, pp. 179–221; 57, pp. 4–23. For Anglo-Catholicism he limits himself almost exclusively to the Oxford Conference of 1899.

[8] Cf. *Irenikon*, 38 (1965), pp. 370–71; *ibid.*, 39 (1966), pp. 393–95.

[9] On the "Inter-Orthodox Commission of Belgrade on Anglicanism", we can avail ourselves of two complementary contributions. The articles of Professor Trembelas appeared in *Ekklesia* between October 1, 1966 and April 15, 1967. They were assembled in the book by the same author, *He en Beligradio Pan-orthodoxos Theologike Epitrope* (Athens, 1967). The other contribution is the article of Bishop Basil, "La Commission inter-orthodoxe pour le dialogue avec les Anglicans (Belgrade, September

two lines of thought took shape. One line of thought was represented by Metropolitan Athenagoras of Thyatira (Ecumenical Patriarchate) and the Romanian delegates; the other, which was more reserved and cautious, was represented by Russia and Greece. The other Churches sided with one of these two viewpoints or took some midway position. The differences derived mainly from differing evaluations of Anglicanism.

Viewpoints Expressed

The president of the Commission, Athenagoras of Thyatira (Great Britain) accepted the Anglo-Catholic interpretation and proposed to support it by recognizing its sacraments and, above all, the validity of its hierachy.

Metropolitan Justin (Moldavia) stressed the Bucharest agreements and read the decision of the Romanian Synod on them. All the previous accords, and particularly those of 1935, should be accepted by all the Orthodox; this was true also for the validity of those ordinations examined at Bucharest. While that conference had considered them "under certain conditions", the Metropolitan felt that these conditions had been met in the agreements which resulted from those meetings. Bishop Anthime was positive on the question of validity.

The stricter tendency showed up in the presentations of the Russian representatives. Bishop Basil Krivocheine stressed the existence of other tendencies in Anglicanism and the absence of a single unified doctrine. Even when one limited the considerations to sacramental questions, "the differences are of such magnitude that it would be very difficult, in the present state of affairs, to recognize the validity of the hierarchy". The question had never been discussed by all the Orthodox Churches together, and it had to be taken up.

The other delegate of the Moscow Church, Liverij Voronov, reiterated the main points of his 1964 paper.

1–15, 1966)," *Messager de l'exarchat russe en Europe occidentale,* 58 (1967), pp. 74–106. These articles are based on the Proceeding of the Commission, which they cite.

Representing the Greek Church, Professor Bratsiotis gave a brief survey of Anglicanism that was consistent with his 1939 memorandum: there was nothing to be said against the Anglican ritual, but there was great doctrinal variety. He also examined the absence of unanimous agreement among the Anglicans regarding the Bucharest agreements of 1936–37. Ecclesiology had to be a central topic in any dialogue, and there was need to discuss ordinations and the points of Bucharest along with Anglican tendencies.[10]

Professor Trembelas, representing the Church of Jerusalem which had recognized the validity of Anglican orders in 1923, picked up the theme of Anglican *comprehensiveness* that he had discussed in 1939.[11]

Discussion

These seven reports led to a general discussion. The Churches which had not been heard from offered their opinions. Gradually the lines of opposition began to form between the views of Bishop Basil (Russian Church) and Bishop Justin (Romania).

Metropolitan Nicodemus of Sliven (Bulgaria), who had been rather pro-Anglican at the Moscow meeting of 1948, objected that "the Anglicans were being attacked without being present themselves". However, he also felt that Metropolitan Justin was too categorical; the Anglican position would have to be examined very closely. In this connection, he read a declaration of the Bulgarian Synod.[12]

[10] The report of Professor Bratsiotis (September 9) appeared in *Ekklesia* (May, 1967), pp. 223–27. He has also republished his report of 1939 with several additions: Bratsiotis, *Hai Anglikanikai Cheirotoniai Ex Epopseos Orthodoxou* (Athens, 2 1966) (with the comments of Professor Trembelas on "comprehensiveness", *ibid.*, pp. 53–55).

[11] The observations and commentaries of Professor Trembelas (see footnote 9) have been studied by a Greek-American theologian: R. Stephanopoulos, "Reactions to the Belgrade Resolution," in *St. Vladimir's Seminary Quarterly*, 11 (1967), pp. 100–03. I should also point out that Professor Trembelas found the Russian statements "extremely conservative".

[12] Survey of opinions on the sacraments, the tendency of the Anglican Church, value of the 39 Articles, the problem of intercommunion with

Alexandria, which had recognized Anglican orders in 1930, was relatively favorable. Metropolitan Parthenios of Carthage felt that some decision should be reached on this question, on which the Orthodox Churches had no single, united opinion. Professor Konidaris of Athens, an Alexandrian delegate, felt that they should not allow the present situation to go on, with only some of the Orthodox Churches recognizing Anglican validity; he suggested that the reasons behind the decision of these Churches should be sent to all the Orthodox Churches by the Patriarch of Constantinople.

The Bishop of Thyatira read a brief report, pointing out that both the points of agreement and disagreement had been clearly brought out. This led to a new exchange between Bishop Basil and Bishop Justin. The former stressed the differing ideas on the present status of Anglicanism, noting that the discussions on orders had never been "Pan-Orthodox". Bishop Justin replied that the Orthodox Churches had reached an agreement with the Anglicans and that this agreement could not be annulled. The accords of 1936 had been confirmed by the Synod in 1936 and again in 1966. These questions could no longer be the topic of a Pan-Orthodox conference.

Bishop Basil replied that the Russian Church respected the Bucharest dialogues, but that these dialogues could not force a commitment on Orthodoxy as a whole. New discussions would have to take place before a dialogue was opened with Anglicanism.

Finland (N. Karioma) was quite negative on the question. Czechoslovakia left open the questions. Bishop Nicholas of Preshov proposed this theme: "the reestablishment of the ecumenical validity of Anglican orders and of eucharistic unity with Orthodoxy." Radivoy Jakovlevic supported the Romanians, but "to the extent that other autocephalous Churches had not accepted the viewpoint of the Romanian Church", it would be useful if the validity of Anglican orders were taken as the theme

Old Catholics, Lutherans (Swedish) and Methodists. Cf. Trembelas, *op. cit.*, pp. 154–5.

for discussion. The Churches which had approved the validity of Anglican orders obviously had sound reasons for doing so; at the same time, however, the articles of Professor Voronov made a profound impression upon him. The ultimate decision would have to be left up to the Holy Spirit.

Professor Mihalof of Preshov noted that the Moscow Conference of 1948 had not ruled out the possibility of recognizing Anglican orders, but that it had made such recognition dependent on certain conditions. The Churches which had already recognized their validity should send their conclusions to the Ecumenical Patriarch for study by the other Churches.

Serbia took a very progressive approach. Bishop Stephen of Dalmatia pointed out that prior conferences and the decisions of individual Churches should be taken into account on the question of validity. "I think that our sister-Church of Romania has made the greatest contribution in this area, and that there is nothing in the Bucharest agreements that cannot be accepted. We certainly cannot say that all the Orthodox Churches have avoided communicating with the Anglican Churches, that they have not recognized in them the signs of 'ecclesiality'. When Anglican bishops visit us, our Churches accord them the insignias of the episcopate, thus recognizing in practice the orders which they bear. We must not be inconsistent on this question." [13]

The other delegate, Professor Mitsidis, noted the differences among the Orthodox Churches and expressed his hope that they would be resolved with charity and consideration. Finally, Bishop Epiphanius tried to correct any erroneous impressions left by Professor Trembelas, a delegate from Jerusalem. Bishop Epiphanius asserted this: "I declare officially that the Church of Jerusalem recognized Anglican orders one year after the Church

---

[13] In the restricted sense of 1923, however, for he went on to say: "This recognition does not mean that we would accept Anglican ordinations (*in se*?) because that would involve some sort of intercommunion. Such intercommunion would be inconceivable without the prior agreement of all the Orthodox Churches." Cf. Trembelas, *op. cit.*, p. 162. On the connection between recognition *in se* and intercommunion, in the view of some Greek theologians, see J. Kotsonis, *The Validity of Anglican Orders* (Brookline, Mass., 1958), p. 38.

of Constantinople did, and in the same sense. This patriarchate will continue to recognize them, with a view toward future union with the Anglican Church."

The Decision

After these discussions, an editorial committee drew up the list of topics for the dialogue. The first category concerned subjects on which there had been agreements between the Anglicans and certain Orthodox Churches (the one at Bucharest, for example). This included the validity of Anglican orders and related questions. In contrast to the topics in the three other categories, these topics are to be excluded from Pan-Orthodox discussions "for the present" (an addition which Bishop Basil requested from Bishop Justin). These topics, however, can be the subject of bilateral discussions between the Anglicans and one or another autocephalous Orthodox Church, as Bishop Basil Krivocheine had suggested.[14]

VI

AN ANGLO-RUSSIAN DIALOGUE: NOVEMBER 1966

Out of this came a meeting at Lambeth from November 1–11, 1966. It was an unofficial meeting between a small group of Orthodox representatives, headed by Bishop Basil, and a similar group of Anglicans headed by Dr. H. Carpenter, the Bishop of Oxford.[15] For the first time the Russian Church discussed the question of validity directly with the Anglicans.

The Russian delegation had been given instructions by their Holy Synod (October 8). It declared that the Russian Orthodox

[14] For a critique of this distinction, see Trembelas, *op. cit.*, pp. 168–9. The full text of the Belgrade Resolution with all details can be found in Basil, *op. cit.*, 102–06.

[15] The other Russian delegates were Bishop Vladimir of Zvenigorod, Archpriest Vitalij Borovoy, and Archbishop Antonij Bloom. For the Anglicans: Bishop of Quincy (Dr. Francis Lickfield), Dr. Paul Anderson of the Episcopalian Church of the United States, and Dr. T. M. Parker of the University of Oxford.

Church had not taken a definitive position on the validity of Anglican orders, because such a position would depend on Anglican doctrine on related topics. Russian theologians had to find out whether Orthodox doctrine on the priesthood, the eucharist and apostolic succession (Bucharest agreement, 1935) corresponded with authentic Anglican doctrine, not just with a doctrine accepted in Anglicanism.[16]

In an article that has just now appeared,[17] we find that Dr. Carpenter, replying in his own name, answered these questions of the Russian delegation in the latter sense. But let me point out that such interchanges will go on. I think that within Anglicanism, where certain formulations have become hard and fast with the passage of time, there will be a convergence toward the traditional view. It will become more apparent as time goes on, thanks to the renewed theological and liturgical efforts that are now taking place within Anglicanism.[18]

[16] *Zhurnal Moskovskoy Patriarchii* (1966), p. 4.

[17] Archbishop Basil, "Bogoslovskie sobesedovanya po voprochu ob anglicanskom svyascenstve mezhdu anglikanskoy i russkoy pravoslavnoi cerkvami," in *Zhurnal Moskovskoy Patriarchii,* 17 (1967), pp. 45–53.

[18] The joint Catholic-Episcopalian Commission reached the conclusion (May, 1967) that "the notion of eucharistic sacrifice was no longer an obstacle between the two Churches". Cf. the text in *Irenikon* (1967).

PART III
DOCUMENTATION
CONCILIUM

Office of the Executive Secretary
Nijmegen, Netherlands

Concilium General Secretariat/*Nijmegen, Netherlands*

Women's Place in the Ministry of Non-Catholic Christian Churches

A survey of the actual line taken by the various Churches[1] with regard to the admission of women to office and the theological justification of their position shows at first sight a rapid development toward the complete acceptance of women in ecclesiastical office. This favorable turn of events is mainly due to some four factors which we wish to recall before we can situate, in the second part of this article, the various opinions of the Churches about women in office.

I

THE FACTORS THAT HAVE HAD A BEARING ON THE POSITION OF WOMEN IN THE MINISTRY

1. *The Way in Which "Office" Is Understood*

A convincing survey of the rather divergent points of view

[1] In the final stages of this documentation the General Secretariat received some written suggestions from Prof. Dr. H. van der Linde of Nijmegen University and some oral corrections during a discussion with the following women ministers: Dr. Jongeling; Dr. G. Rikin-Bijleveld; Dr. T. Scholten-van Iterson and Dr. W. Timmermans. As space does not allow for a detailed bibliography we refer to the convenient *Woman and Holy Orders, Being the Report of a Commission Appointed by the Archbishops of Canterbury and York* (London, 1966) and the there given bibliography (pp. 40–4). We also thank the Secretariat of the World Council of Churches at Geneva for the information provided.

on this issue in the various Christian Churches makes one immediately aware of a difficulty. The Orthodox, Anglican or Protestant Churches hold very different views on the ecclesiastical
office. The reader may have noticed this already in the preceding
contributions by van Ruler, Dupuy, Marot and Chadwick. For
the Orthodox and the Anglicans the office is a sacrament; it is
"sacred", comes from on high, from God, and is instituted by
Christ. For most Protestants the office is not a sacrament; it
comes from below, from the call of the community in which they
see the call of God. For many it is something that has grown as
a social and obvious necessity. It is easy to see that, in the case
of the Orthodox and the Anglicans, the structure of the office
easily becomes rigid and static, does not easily deviate from the
old established pattern, and emphasizes succession and ordination. In the case of the Protestants, the atmosphere is more easily
open to a certain evolution of the office; they do not consider
themselves so rigidly bound by tradition and are inclined to attach
more importance to proven ability than validity of ordination.
When they first look at the issue of women in office, they will
attach great importance to Tradition and Scripture, while the
second group will emphasize the signs of the time and the growing appreciation of woman's gifts. Hence, there will be stronger
objections to woman's place in the ministry among Orthodox and
Anglicans than among Protestants. To this one must add that for
the Orthodox and Anglicans the ministry embraces far more
than is the case in Protestant Churches. For the Protestants the
function of preaching the Gospel is the sole divine function
(*ministerium divinum*). It has been lifted out of the sphere of
the "sacred"; by virtue of the universal priesthood (1 Pet. 2, 9)
the faithful form, through their bond with Christ the High Priest,
a people of priests and there is no distinction between priesthood
and laity. For Luther all the faithful are "priests and bishops".[2]
For Orthodox and Anglicans, closer to the Catholic type of
Church, the divine ministry contains also the priestly functions
and the jurisdictional functions of government. This adds to the

[2] W.A. 6, p. 407.

difficulties when the place of woman is considered. It is easier to admit woman to the office of preaching than to the administration of the sacraments or the functions of government. In a very general way one may say that a "Low Church" view of the ministry is more favorable to woman than a "High Church" view.

2. *The Change in the Appreciation of Woman*

The idea that woman is no longer the "second" sex, that she is man's equal in modern society, that the division between male and female careers seems to be overcome and that sexual discrimination has been abandoned for an evangelical humanization of the sexes, has made it more obvious that woman's place in ecclesiastical office deserves to be taken seriously. "Man and woman are not mutually hostile, mutually exclusive or mutually isolating, but mutually enriching and complementary. That is why we cannot really speak of the problem of 'women', not even in this matter of office, but of a human problem that concerns man and woman equally. As long as this is not realized woman remains 'the other' and man is the human being." [3] However, enough has been said about this in the articles by Gössmann and Peters. Here we have only to point out that this change in appreciation is again more effective in the "Low Church" than in the "High Church", more in the smaller than in the larger Churches.

3. *The Collapse of the Theological Arguments*

As the changed circumstances forced the various Churches to reconsider their position with regard to the previously "obvious" exclusion of woman from Church office, they had to take a new look at the arguments for or against. The result has been that the arguments for man's exclusive right to office proved unconvincing or so tied up with past cultures that modern man could no longer appreciate them or a mere rationalization of subconscious emotions. Thus the Anglican report on the place of woman in the ministry said: "When the possibility of an important change

[3] T. Govaart-Halkes, in *Kosmos en Oecumene* 1, 2, 48 (1967).

touches on powerful and sometimes subconscious anxieties and wishes, intelligent reflection is probably seriously influenced by emotional prejudice." [4] This is particularly true for such "symbolic" arguments as: the minister represents Christ; Christ is a man; therefore only a man can be a minister. Human sciences have made it clear that such arguments conceal emotions concerned with securing the positions of power for man in a culture where his prerogatives are threatened. For many Churches it has become obvious that woman was excluded from the ministry, not for theological reasons, but because men were determined not to allow her in.

4. Ecumenical Considerations

Particularly in those Churches that are members of the World Council the admission of women to the ministry is sometimes blocked by ecumenical considerations: If one Church admits women and another does not, new conflicts will arise that will harm ecumenical progress. Dr. Lukas Vischer points this out in his introduction to *Concerning the Ordination of Woman* (Geneva, 1964), the report sent to the World Council of Churches by the Orthodox, Anglicans and Protestants: "Should precisely such an issue as this not show that the Churches form a community? Can Churches allow their divisions to be perpetuated because they reach different conclusions? Should they not try in every way to come to a common agreement? Should they not at least reach their decisions in living union with other Churches, so that the particular way taken by one Church is at least understood by the others? Churches that refuse to make any concession whatever on this point of woman in the ministry may be tempted to say that those that accept her encourage the division among Christians . . . Should they not envisage the possibility that the direction taken by another Church may be important for themselves? . . . Churches that are prepared to allow woman into the ministry may be tempted to call the others conservative and traditionalist. They may be inclined to attribute it to lack of re-

[4] *Loc. cit.,* p. 46.

spect for woman if one is not even prepared to consider her admission to the ministry . . . If these Churches take the bond of ecumenism seriously, should they not see the importance of continuity in the life of the Church and consider the responsibility of timing the introduction of something new? And does their witness not force them then to express more clearly how they intend to preserve this?"

In the survey of the various positions taken up by the Churches on this point it will become clear that, time and again, one of these factors prevails, while the position is also influenced by the undercurrent of a changing image of the Church. The Orthodox are the most traditional; the Anglicans prefer a pragmatic *via media,* while the Protestants seem to have a relatively open mind on this issue.

II

The Position of the Non-Catholic Christian Churches

1. *The Orthodox*

In the Orthodox Churches one finds everywhere a resolute rejection of the woman's ministry, couched in the most benevolent terms. When one looks for the reason, one always ends up with the assertion: woman has never had a place in the hierarchy, and therefore she cannot have such a place in the future. Modern theology has little influence on such a view; the only thing that seems to be important is the traditional rules of the Church as a whole insofar as these have been laid down in Canon Law and practice. The last word seems to be one of Epiphanius:[5] "Although there is an order of deaconesses, this is not meant for sacerdotal functions or things of that nature . . . Never, since the beginning of the world, has woman served the Lord as a priest"; or that saying of Tertullian:[6] "A woman is not only not

---

[5] *Constitutio Apostolica,* VIII, 6, 28; *Haer.* LXXIX, 3 and XLI, 2.

[6] *De velatione virginum,* IX: "Non permittitur mulieri in ecclesia loqui, sed nec docere, nec tingere, nec offerre, nec illius virilis muneris, necdum sacerdotalis officii sortem sibi vindicare."

allowed to speak in church; she is also not allowed to teach, nor to touch, nor to sacrifice, nor to demand election to this male office and sacerdotal function." Evdokimov,[7] professor at the Orthodox seminary of Paris and one of the best qualified spokesmen for modern Orthodox theology, says many noble things about women but nowhere touches on ecclesiastical or social practice. It is also said that man and woman form together the new reality of the royal priesthood but the actual application of this is written off in a few words. One reads that a woman can be a deaconess but it soon becomes clear that this requires no ordination but only a blessing. It is apparently not yet understood that words like ordination and blessing are of juridical and sacralizing origin, have been introduced later on and that the argument that women receive only a blessing and are therefore not incorporated in a hierarchy exclusively based on ordination, is an argument without any scientific or historical foundation. At the bottom of all this there lies the kind of metaphysical interpretation of woman and the hierarchical view of reality which Gössmann has already dealt with. Moreover, the symbolic argument that Christ was man and that therefore only a man can be priest, is reinforced by another of the same type: Mary was a woman and was not priest; therefore women, seen in the image of Mary, cannot be priests.

However, now that the Orthodox Churches,[8] probably influenced by the World Council of Churches, are prepared to face the question of women's place in the ministry, one may expect a more positive approach there, given the rapid development in other Churches that at first showed grave reservations on the matter.

2. The Anglicans

To the four factors analyzed above, the Anglican position adds a fifth: Anglicans would like to see their orders recognized by

---

[7] P. Evdokimov, La femme et le salut du monde (Paris, 1958).

[8] M. Rinvolucri, Anatomy of a Church. Greek Orthodoxy Today (London, 1966), esp. pp. 92ff. for the new forms of "apostoliki diakonia", such as Zoi and Sotir.

Rome. They are therefore wary of adding to the existing difficulties. Nevertheless, this Church has undergone a tremendous development during the last hundred years which has resulted in a number of new forms of ministry that are open to women. These new forms are in various ways an extension of the already existing function of the deaconess, which exists also in the Orthodox Churches and is to be distinguished from the diaconate. A recent resolution[9] on allowing women to be ordained priests was favorably received by the bishops and the laity, but rejected by the clergy. The pragmatic temperament of the Anglican Church seems to be mainly influenced here by the question of intercommunion with the Methodist and Scandinavian Churches which fully accept the ministry of women and that of maintaining its relations with the Catholic and Orthodox Churches which reject this. The Anglicans seem to refuse to let this issue become an obstacle to ecumenism in any way. It is not likely that women will be admitted to episcopacy and priesthood in the near future, but it is possible that the diaconate will be reformed in such a way as to open it up for men and women equally. In the relatively small Presbyterian Church in England, women have been admitted to the ministry already for a long time although it is only recently that the first woman was accepted as a minister because women were not accepted in the Presbyterian seminary. In Scotland the United Free Church has thrown the ministry open to women.

3. *The Protestant Churches*

Among the Protestants it is immediately evident that the more liberal-minded denominations have no difficulty in admitting the ministry of women. Precisely because they are small and have no complicated institutional establishment, they are more elastic and adaptable. These Churches are moreover of the "elite" type with a rather "free-thinking" undercurrent where such questions are solved on the basis of common sense and cultural understanding. Thus the Remonstrant Fraternity accepts the total equality

[9] *Inform. Cath. Intern.,* 292, July 15, 1967.

of man and woman in the ministry. The Baptist community, too, accepts the change in the position of women in modern society and accepts total equality both in principle and in fact. In the larger Churches the question is more complicated. All these larger Churches have in fact a rather influential institutional establishment which decides this issue from above. Once a given community had accepted women in the ministry, the practical difficulties in the lower echelons were overcome soon enough. In general, the weight and kind of objections will depend on the particular type of Church. In the more fundamentalist type, the difficulties arise from particular scriptural texts, but then, the same Scripture eliminates all discrimination between man and woman in Galatians 3, 28. Churches that stress continuity with the early Church will at first see an insuperable difficulty in succession and tradition, but the same tradition also shows up the historicity of the ministry. Where, as in the presbyterial type of Churches, the God-willed principle of ordination created some difficulty at the start, the principle of a mutually complementary partnership between man and woman soon introduced woman into the ministry. Where many missionary Churches at first followed the mother Church in this question, the freedom from the burden of history and tradition soon worked in favor of women. Thus there are already women preachers in some Indonesian Churches. They are numerous in Japan, and in Liberia the first woman-preacher has been appointed.

In theory all these Churches show a tendency to open up all ecclesiastical functions to women. In practice one can observe a kind of gradation in this process: women are accepted in the Church's service but this service is still distinct from the ministry; a distinction is made between various functions of the ministry and women are accepted as "elders", deaconesses, and preach as assistants to a preacher. This implies that she can also function at the Lord's supper. She is admitted to all functions but under supervision of a male colleague. She is admitted fully to all functions but with corresponding differentiations. She is admitted to all functions but limited in the actual exercise to special circumstances (e.g., emergency regions), to the sick or to the young at school. The actual admission is therefore only gradual. If the ministry of a woman is accepted, there is still the question of *how far* she is admitted. In Germany where every locally established Church (*Landeskirche*) determines its own attitude on this point, a woman is fully accepted as pastor, particularly in the United Church (*Unierte Kirche*), but she can only be called upon in communities where one or more male preachers are operating. In Scandinavia where the Lutheran Church is the Established Church, Parliament opened up the ministry for women but this is fiercely opposed by the Churches, particularly in "High Church" circles that want to maintain intercommunion with the Anglican Churches. In the United States the most important Presbyterian Church, the United Presbyterian Church, admits both men and women to the ministry on equal terms. Women preachers are active in various Swiss *Landeskirchen* although the decision was reached with great difficulty. At the Synod of May 2, 1966, the Reformed Church in France accepted the ministry of women. Of the 168 Churches that belonged in 1958 to the World Council of Churches, 48 had admitted women to the full ministry. The number is higher today.

As in the emancipation of women, we can also discern two phases in this present issue. There is a first phase during which a very small number of women commit themselves consciously to an ideal that in practice amounts to the achievement of a few clearly defined goals: education for girls, access to various careers and the training for those careers, the suffrage (both active and passive), abolition of all discrimination in law or in pay. These aims have their counterparts on women's long way to the ministry.[10] The achievement of these aims is not the end. It must be followed by a more laborious second phase: partnership of man and woman in ecclesiastical office in a way that does not create a

[10] *Compte rendu de la conférence internationale oecuménique féminine —la femme chrétienne co-artisane d'une société en évolution* (Taizé, 1967), pp. 68–9; C. M. van Asch van Wijck, "Man en vrouw: een literatuuroverzicht," in *Wending* 21, pp. 323–37; R. J. A. van Eyden, "Die Frau im Kirchenamt," in *Wort und Wahrheit* 22, 5 (1967), pp. 350–62.

loss of religious value on the one hand and does not become clericalized on the other.

In conclusion we append a survey of the actual situation in some 60 Churches representing the three types mentioned above. Most data come from the World Council of Churches and date from 1963. The interest does not lie so much in the statistics as in the line of development.

	DENOMINA-TION	IS ISSUE RELEVANT?	MINISTRY OPEN TO WOMAN?	TO WHAT EXTENT?	SINCE WHEN?
1.	American Baptist Convention	Yes. With material for study	Yes	Same as for men	?
2.	American Lutheran Church	No—no problem	No	Only as deaconess for visiting and teaching	?
3.	Anglican Church of Canada	Yes	No	Only as deaconess for pastoral jobs	?
4.	Anglican Church of Uganda	No	No	Start is made with training for social work	1965
5.	Anglican Church of West Indies	No, against tradition	No	Sisters Companions of Jesus are active	?
6.	Associated Churches of Christ in New Zealand	No, but no objections made	Yes in theory; not yet in practice	Full equality is possible; there are deaconesses	?
7.	Baptist Union of Gr. Britain and Ireland	Yes, with material for study	Yes	Same as for men, but few places; more for deaconesses	1918
8.	Baptist Union of New Zealand	No, but no obstruction	Yes in theory but no training	In principle as for men; there are deaconesses	1958
9.	Church of England	Yes; study commission set up 1963	Not as bishop, priest or deacon	As deaconesses: various religious communities	Report of 1966 is more positive
10.	Church of the Brethren, U.S.A.	Yes; solution is obvious	Yes	As for men; moreover deaconesses (not ordained)	1960
11.	Church of Augsburg Confession of Strasbourg	Yes, and actually solved	Yes	Same as men in pastoral work if they renounce marriage and have theological training	1960 (Consistoire supérieur)
12.	Church of England in Australia	Yes	No	Deaconesses	From the start
13.	Church of Ireland	No	No	Teaching and welfare	From the start
14.	Church of the Province of New Zealand	Yes, in some cases	No	Deaconesses and sisters	From the start
15.	Church of the Prov. of South Africa	No	No	Some indigenous communities	From the start
16.	Church of Scotland	No, custom and tradition followed	No, but 7 women ordained in other Churches	Deaconesses since 1888	1564 (Knox)

	DENOMINA-TION	IS ISSUE RELE-VANT?	MINIS-TRY OPEN TO WOM-AN?	TO WHAT EXTENT?	SINCE WHEN?
17.	Church of South India	Yes	No	55 Sisters in a religious order	From the start
18.	Church of Sweden	Since 1957, solved by Parliamentary decree, 1958	Yes, but bishop cannot be forced to ordain woman	Same status and rights as man ("präst")	1959
19.	Church in Wales	Not studied	No	Deaconesses, sisters and welfare workers	From the start
20.	Congregational Christian Church in Samoa	Yes, no obstacles	No, only men are theologically trained	Deaconesses for life with same status as men	From the start
21.	Congregational Union in Australia	Taken as obvious	Yes	All offices and same status as men	1927
22.	Congregational Union of England and Wales	Solved	Yes	Same status and privileges as men	1917
23.	Congregational Union of Scotland	Solved	Yes	Same status as men for ministry of Word and sacrament	1929
24.	Eglise chrétienne missionaire belge	No; not asked for	No	Only women missionaries	?
25.	Eglise évangélique luthérienne de France	No basic study made	Not as a rule; some exceptions	One woman has a parish	?
26.	Eglise Réformée de France	Since study commission of 1961	Yes	Same status as man	1949; approved in 1965
27.	Estonian Evangelical Lutheran Church	Twice put on agenda	No; no local demand	Two women preachers, but not ordained	?
28.	Estonian Evangelical Lutheran Church in Exile	Not officially	No	Question does not arise	—
29.	Evangelical Church of Augsburg Confession (Poland)	Not popular	No	Deaconesses and "Church teaching", no ordination	—
30.	Ev. Church of Augsburg Conf. (Romania)	Does not arise	No	Other services undertaken by State	—
31.	Ev. Church of Czech Brethren (Presbyt.)	Solved	Yes	Same status and privileges as pastors and assistants	1953

	DENOMINA-TION	IS ISSUE RELE-VANT?	MINIS-TRY OPEN TO WOM-AN?	TO WHAT EXTENT?	SINCE WHEN?
32.	Ev. Church in New Caledonia and Loyalty Islands	No	No	Formerly deaconesses	—
33.	Ev. Church of N.W. Tanganyika	No	No	Some deaconesses from Germany and Sweden	—
34.	Ev. Lutheran Church in Denmark	Solved by Parliamentary decree 1947	Yes, but bishop decides	Full status and privileges	1947
35.	Ev. Lutheran Church of Iceland	Not studied	No	Some theologically trained women preach	?
36.	Ev. Lutheran Church in the Netherlands	Solved	Yes	Same as for men; also deaconesses	1929
37.	Ev. United Brethren Church	Solved long ago	Yes	Same as for men. Of 3,750 ministers 25 are women	—
38.	Evangelische Kirche der Union	Yes	Yes	Full ministry, but must resign on marriage; not same status	—
39.	Friends General Conference	Yes	Yes	Same status as men	From the start
40.	Iglesia Evangélica Española	General opposition	No	—	—
41.	Igreja evangelica de confisas Lutherana no Brasil	Yes	No	Only deaconesses	—
42.	Lutheran Church in America	No interest	No	Deaconesses	1833
43.	Mar Thoma Syrian Church of Malabar	Meaningless	No	Only for evangelization	From the start
44.	Methodist Church of London	Yes	No	Deaconesses	Since Wesley
45.	Methodist Church of U.S.A.	Yes	Yes	Full extent, but there are social barriers	1956
46.	Methodist Church of South America	Solved	Yes	Same status and privileges as men	1960
47.	Methodist Church of Australia	Yes, since 1932	Yes	All functions; special rules for married women	1968
48.	Moravian Church in Gr Britain and Ireland	Yes	Yes	No binding decision in view of practical difficulties	1956
49.	Moravian Church (Northern Prov.) U.S.A.	No	No	Teaching, etc.	For more than 200 years

	DENOMINA-TION	IS ISSUE RELE-VANT?	MINIS-TRY OPEN TO WOM-AN?	TO WHAT EXTENT?	SINCE WHEN?
50.	Moravian Church in Western Cape Prov.	No need	No	White and black home-visiting	—
51.	Nederlands Her-vormde Kerk	Since 1924	Yes	Complete	1967
52.	Orthodox Church in Romania	Forbidden by Scrip-ture and Tradition	No	—	—
53.	Oud Katholieke Kerk in Nederland	Not officially	No	—	—
54.	Patriarchate, Holy Synod	No	No	Only religious	—
55.	Pentecostal Church of Chile	Yes	No	Women ordained as deaconesses have same status as men but may not administer the eu-charist	From the start
56.	Philippine Inde-pendent Church	No; this Church is severed from R.C. Church	No	Deaconesses	—
57.	Presbyterian Church of Aus-tralia	Yes, but not as much as elsewhere	No	Deaconesses for preach-ing and visiting of the sick	1962
58.	Presbyterian Church of Eng-land	Solved	Yes	Same status and privi-leges; deaconesses may administer the Word, not the sacraments	1921
59.	Presb. Church in U.S.A. (South)	Yes	No	—	—
60.	Remonstrantse Broederschap	Solved	Yes	Eligible for all functions	1915 Church Order, a. 145
61.	Russian Orthodox Church	No	No	Can be assistant (starot-sa)	—
62.	Union of Armeni-an Evang. Church-es of Near East	No	No	Men are opposed	—
63.	United Church of Christ (U.S.A.)	Solved	Yes	No restrictions	—
64.	United Church of Christ of Central Africa in Rhodesia	Not studied	No	English and Canadian deaconesses work under supervision of "minister"	—
65.	United Free Church of Scot-land	Solved	Yes	Full extent; in 1960 woman was moderator of General Assembly	1929

66.	United Presbyterian Church in U.S.A.	Solved	Yes	Since women are admitted to full ordination, number of deaconesses declines	1956
67.	Protestants-Evang. Kerk	Since 1924	Yes	Full extent	1965
68.	National Protestant Church of Geneva	Yes	Yes	No restrictions	1967
69.	Austrian Evang. Church of the Augsburg and Helvetian Confession	Yes	Yes	Side by side with male colleagues and in specific functions	1965

BIOGRAPHICAL NOTES

BÉDA RIGAUX, O.F.M.: Born in Belgium in 1899, he was ordained in 1923. He studied at Louvain, receiving his doctorate and licentiate in theology. He was provincial of his Order in Belgium from 1945 to 1951. Since 1956 he has been professor of religious studies at the Institute Superieur of Louvain University. His published works include *Témoignage sur l'Evangile de St. Matthieu* (Tournai, 1967).

ANTONIO JAVIERRE, S.D.B.: Born in Spain in 1921, he was ordained in 1949. He studied at the University of Salamanca, at the Gregorian and at Louvain, obtaining his doctorate in theology in 1951. He is professor of fundamental theology at the Salesian Atheneum in Rome, where he is also dean of the faculty of theology. His publications include *Promoción conciliar del diálogo ecumenico* (Madrid 1966) and *El tema literario de la sucesión. Prolegómenos para el estudio de la sucesión apostólica* (Zurich 1963).

HANS KÜNG: Born in Switzerland in 1928, he was ordained in 1954. He studied at the Gregorian, at the Catholic Institute in Paris and at the Sorbonne, receiving his doctorate in theology in 1957. He is professor of dogmatic and ecumenical theology at the University of Tübingen, where he is also director of the Institute of Ecumenical Theology. Among his important publications are *Structures of the Church* (London, 1965), *Justification* (London, 1965), and *The Church* (London and New York, 1967).

JOHANNES REMMERS: Born in the Netherlands in 1913, he was ordained in 1938. He studied at the Major Seminary at Haaren, at the Oriental Institute in Rome, and at the University of Nijmegen. He received his doctorate in theology and in Eastern Church studies in 1949. Since 1964 he has been professor of the history and theology of the Eastern Churches at Münster University, where he is also director of the Catholic Ecumenical Institute. His published works include *Het oecumenisch gesprek tussen Orthodoxie en Katholicisme* (Nijmegen, 1964).

AVERY DULLES, S.J.: Born in America in 1918, he was ordained in 1956. He studied at Harvard and Woodstock College, and in Rome at the Gregorian, obtaining degrees in arts and philosophy as well as a doctorate in theology in 1960. He has been professor of systematic theology at Woodstock College since 1960, and adviser to the Secretariat for Non-Believers since 1966. His publications include *Apologetics and the Biblical Christ* (London 1964).

ARNOLD VAN RULER: Born in the Netherlands in 1908, he is a member of the Dutch Reformed Church. He is a doctor of theology, and holds the posts of professor of biblical theology, Christian ethics and history of the Dutch Reformed Church at the University of Utrecht. He is also a member of the Synod of the Dutch Reformed Church. Among his published works are *Die christliche Kirche und das Alte Testament* (Munich, 1955), and *Reformatorische opmerkingen in de ontmoeting met Rome* (Hilversum-Anvers, 1965).

BERNARD DUPUY, O.P.: Born in Paris in 1925, he was ordained in 1955. He studied at the Ecole Polytechnique in Paris and at the faculties of philosophy and theology of the Saulchoir, where he obtained his degree in theology. He has taught fundamental theology and ecclesiology at the Saulchoir since 1959. A *peritus* at Vatican Council II, he is the author of *L'Épiscopat et l'Église Universelle* (Paris, 1962).

MAURICE VILLAIN, S.M.: Born in France in 1900, he was ordained in 1927. He studied at the Sorbonne, at the Ecole des Chartes in Paris, and at the Theological Faculty in Lyons, receiving his doctorate in theology in 1929. He has held professorships of dogma and ecclesiology in Belgium and France. His publications include *Introduction a l'Oecumenisme* (Paris, 1964) and *Vatican II et le dialogue oecumenique* (Paris, 1966).

JOSEPH DUSS-VON WERDT: Born in Switzerland in 1932, he studied at the Philosophical Institute of Louvain University and at the Faculty of Theology of Munich, receiving doctorates in philosophy in 1957 and in theology in 1964. He is a member of the editorial board of the review *Ehe* (Tübingen-Berne) and co-director of the Institute of Marriage and Family Guidance at Zurich. He collaborated with L. M. Weber on *Gewissensfreiheit?* (Mainz 1966).

ELIZABETH GÖSSMANN: Born in Germany in 1928, she received her doctorate in theology in 1954, and since 1955 has combined her career as a writer in Germany with that of Dean of the philosophy and theology faculties at two universities in Tokyo. Her publications include *Die Frau und ihr Auftrag* (Freiburg-im-Breisgau, 1965) and *Das Bild der Frau heute* (Dusseldorf, 1967).

JAN PETERS, O.C.D.: Born in the Netherlands in 1921, he was ordained in 1946. He studied at Louvain and Nijmegen, obtaining his doctorate in theology in 1957. He was professor of dogma and spirituality at the Theologicum of the Discalced Carmelites at Smakt-Venray from 1949 to 1966, where he was also Dean of Studies from 1957 to 1966. He is now theological adviser to *Concilium,* a member of the Pastoral Council of the Netherlands and secretary of the Scientific Society of Dutch Catholic Theologians. Among his publications are *Geloof en mystiek. Een theologische bezinning op de geestelijke werken van St. Jan van het Kruis* (Louvain, 1957), *Volledige werken van de H. Johannes van het Kruis* (Hilversum-Anvers, 1963), and *God tegemoet* (Hilversum-Anvers, 1963).

HENRY CHADWICK: Born in England in 1920, he was ordained in the Anglican Church in 1944. He studied at Cambridge University, receiving his doctorate in theology in 1957. He is a Fellow of the British Academy and holds honorary degrees of the universities of Glasgow and Uppsala. He has been a professor of theology at Oxford University since 1959. His publications include *Early Christian Thought and the Classical Tradition.*

HILAIRE MAROT, O.S.B.: Born in 1920, he became a Benedictine, and pursued his studies at the University of Paris and at the Collegio San Anselmo in Rome, earning degrees in theology and history. He is a regular contributor to various reviews, notably *Irenikon,* and has contributed to several symposia.

International Publishers of CONCILIUM

ENGLISH EDITION
Paulist Press
Glen Rock, N. J., U.S.A.

Burns & Oates Ltd.
25 Ashley Place
London, S.W.1

DUTCH EDITION
Uitgeverij Paul Brand, N. V.
Hilversum, Netherlands

FRENCH EDITION
Maison Mame
Tours/Paris, France

JAPANESE EDITION (PARTIAL)
Nansôsha
Tokyo, Japan

GERMAN EDITION
Verlagsanstalt Benziger & Co., A.G.
Einsiedeln, Switzerland

Matthias Grunewald-Verlag
Mainz, W. Germany

SPANISH EDITION
Ediciones Guadarrama
Madrid, Spain

PORTUGUESE EDITION
Livraria Morais Editora, **Ltda.**
Lisbon, Portugal

ITALIAN EDITION
Editrice Queriniana
Brescia, Italy